TRUSTING WOMEN

TRUSTING WOMEN

*The Way of Women
in Churches of Christ*

Billie Silvey, Editor

New
Leaf
Books
Orange, California

TRUSTING WOMEN
published by New Leaf Books

Copyright 2002 by Billie Silvey

ISBN 0-9714289-2-1
Printed in the United States of America

Cover design by Kristy McTaggert, The ColorEdge, Costa Mesa, CA

For information:
New Leaf Books, 12542 S. Fairmont, Orange, CA 92869
1-877-634-6004 (toll free)

www.newleafbooks.org

02 03 04 05 06 07   9 8 7 6 5 4 3 2 1

Contents

Introduction

The role of women in the church. We speak of it as if all women did—or wanted to do—the same things. Why does no one discuss the role of men in the church? Because that would be ridiculous. Men do all kinds of things in the church. Some preach, some teach, some lead singing, some pray, some read scripture, some usher, some fill communion trays or count the contribution or teach children or chaperone teens. Some work as missionaries, visit the sick, edit books and magazines, feed the hungry or work with prisoners.

Women are just as diverse. As the writers in this book indicate, we are used by God in a wide variety of ministries. Some of our differences are based on our differing ages. Women who came of age before the Women's Movement of the 1970s may be content with more traditional roles. Or we may be in the habit of filling them or concerned about the risk of being divisive and "rocking the boat." Or we may just lack the imagination of our younger sisters.

Other differences stem from our varied geographic locations. Some parts of the country may be more "on the cutting edge" than others. Small towns may be more conservative than large cities—or vice versa.

Our views of what God is calling each of us to do in his service vary according to the gifts he's given us, our innate tendencies and the activities that bring us joy and satisfaction.

For whatever reasons, we are very different. There is no single voice that is women's voice in Churches of Christ in these early years of the twenty-first century. But there are also many ways that we are alike. In fact, in editing this volume, I was at least as struck by our similarities as by our differences. Each writer has a simple faith in God—a trust that God is in charge of her life and is directing it to his own ends. Each has a rich prayer life, and a commitment to God's Word, his church and his timing. And each of us believes that God has given us gifts to use in his service.

Each of us recognizes a debt, not just to God, but to the people in our lives—people who have mentored and encouraged us in our walk. If we ask anything of the men—and other women—in our lives, it is trust. We trust God to lead us, and we are growing to trust ourselves to know and do his will. We ask that others trust us and trust God's Spirit within us. Trust us to recognize God's voice as we discover our own. We'll make mistakes and fall short. All of us do. But we've learned and will continue to learn as we grow in grace and under-standing of God's will for our lives.

Some may feel, as I have felt, that our discussions of the women's issue have distracted us from serving God in ways we already know he desires. But anything that causes us to search the scriptures, to think and to pray can bless the church and us as individuals. May God bring a special blessing to each of us as he leads us through this foment to a closer walk with him.

Billie Silvey

1

'Backwards and in High Heels'

Lindy Adams

Ginger Rogers, Fred Astaire's famous dance partner, once said something to the effect that she had danced all the complex steps Fred Astaire had mastered so brilliantly, only "backwards and in high heels."

That is the way I feel sometimes about my journey as a woman through the Churches of Christ. I have no complaint against the many men who encouraged me, mentored me, taught me, inspired me. They encouraged my growth and accomplishments at every turn.

But finding the right spots for my talents and finding ways to achieve once in those spots demanded I do all my male counterparts did, only "backwards and in high heels." And literally, as far as the high heels were concerned.

Many women harbor terrible hurts and memories of repression from the various men in their early—and present day—lives in Churches of Christ. I am one of the fortunate ones who in large part escaped that.

But although I relished the attention, encouragement and affirmation I received over the years from the men in my life in the church, none shed light on how I would use my gifts and talents while maintaining a home, raising a family and holding a job. Of course, women of my generation (I'm now 52) were charting new waters. Few women before had tried to do it all, as I and many of my compatriots were attempting. So perhaps these mentors advised not because they knew not, since few women had attempted it before. Or perhaps because the question never occurred to them.

Early Influences

My father, a Southern gentleman and Restoration Movement aristocrat of sorts—his great-grandfather was baptized by Barton W. Stone—relished the accomplishments of his three daughters and was particularly proud of our academic achievements. Although he and my mother had a conventional marriage, typical of the post-World War II era, and Daddy was fond of saying he was the "head of the house" and of being quite domineering at times, in reality he was a man whose innate integrity and affirming love provided a secure backdrop for growing up. It was my dad who explained to me that the trouble with Churches of Christ was that they promoted a religion of laws, while Christianity is inherently a religion of principles.

The first minister I remember hearing was Carroll Ellis, beloved Lipscomb speech professor, at my home congregation, Chapel Avenue. His daughter Mufti was my age and the absolute apple of his eye. As I spent a fair amount of time at the Ellis home next to the Lipscomb campus on Rosemont Avenue, I enjoyed his benign appreciation and admiration for all the interesting women who crossed his path—of whom his wife Tottie was chief.

As I traveled on to Lipscomb Junior High and High School, our complex principal Damon Daniel instilled in us the principle that "nothing Christian is inferior," a worthy challenge in some ways, but a terrible curse for students already prone to be compulsive over-achievers. And although I was forced to serve as class secretary for three years and student body secretary my senior year because women students weren't allowed to run for president, my cohorts and I competed and achieved in all sorts of ways.

It is hard to remember what a different time it was—a time when a Sunday afternoon might be spent at a tea or "chocolate" at a class-mate's home, with the girls and boys attending in their Sunday best—

whiling away the time by balancing crystal plates and cups on their laps and making polite conversation.

A time when my mother—who her daughters felt was a Katharine Hepburn kind of woman trapped in a pleasantly conventional life— busied herself running the model of a highly efficient household with four children while providing an abundance of love and plenty of time for sharing a glass of iced tea and discussing every facet of life— great and small. Mamma was often chagrined that her only option for service in the church was to "bake cakes" as she termed it. All of us were gratified when Mamma finished college in her 50s and found her voice as a leader in the restoration of historic homes on the Lipscomb campus.

But of course, in that day there were plenty of oppressive and repressive men around—the brilliant Athens Clay Pullias comes to mind, who exerted as much control and dominance over our campus and everyone on it as possible.

But in our sequestered secondary school world on the back side of the campus near the Granny White church and Mayfair Avenue, all the students—including the women—flourished under the tutelage of outstanding teachers. The exacting and much admired Martha Riedl, who certainly expected no less of her women students than the men, was assigned to teach us English beginning in the ninth grade because so many faculty and administrative offspring were in our class. Those with the molding and shaping duties knew Mrs. Riedl, the recent vale- dictorian of Lipscomb College, would prepare us well for the college of our choice—preferably Lipscomb.

This she began early by designing a first exam in which she test- ed us on the content of the footnotes in Shakespeare's *As You Like It*. Duly chastised by our poor grades, we spent the next four years striv- ing to meet her standards.

And Mrs. Riedl was not alone. Besides Principal Daniel's provoca- tive Bible class, which covered everything from how many times a day a girl should brush her hair to make it shine to the weightier matters of the law, we studied under esteemed Lipscomb professor Dennis Loyd, who told us his goal was to put us on name-dropping terms with the greatest in literature, art and contemporary culture, and the kindly Harold Lipford who, with the openness of his West Texas roots, loved us, patiently directed our terrible theatrical productions and taught us to sing well while standing straight and looking good, complete with the requisite dyed-to-match satin pumps.

But no one even hinted that women shouldn't achieve, and outstanding women students were often named newspaper and yearbook editors, prestigious roles at Lipscomb.

What were women supposed to do with this marvelous training? Well, go to college, of course. But if anyone thought through what women were then to do with their degrees in accounting or biochemistry, I never heard about it. And the issue of the lack of connection between the education these women received and their options for leadership in the church was not even on the horizon.

Expansive Freedom

From Lipscomb, I moved 700 miles across the country to attend Oklahoma Christian College, a fledgling school in the state where my great-grandparents had staked a claim during the famous land runs. Oklahoma was expansive, open and hot, and to a greenhouse flower from Tennessee, it seemed amazingly egalitarian and unpretentious—characteristics I adored. Although I, together with the other female students, endured stricter curfews and rules than the men (who could sneak out at night and eat at one of the truck stops on the highway), things did not seem particularly repressive. Of course this was almost 35 years ago, and we were so square, conventional and straight compared with today that it is hard to envision.

A strange irony of the Oklahoma experience for my lifelong friends who shared it was that, in this raw state and raw college, we found incredible intellectual liberation. And this under President James O. Baird, known by some for his repression and domination.

The scholarly Bailey McBride, the ultimate mentor of Oklahoma Christian students and alumni, enthralled us as he held forth on Shakespeare, Faulkner and literary criticism. And the amazing scholar, thinker and questioner Harold Fletcher proved to be a wellspring of intellectual and theological freedom. It was Harold Fletcher who had a much-discussed subversive cartoon posted on his door showing a man carrying a box labeled "truth." The caption read, "Well, now I've got it."

The Fletchers—Harold and Mary Helen and their children—modeled a much emulated lifestyle which combined the best of today's touted "family values" with great openness of thought and discussion and a wonderful element of travel, music and the arts. It was the Fletchers who loved and mentored the college's African-American students and supported the Human Relations Forum, the leaders of which engaged in Oklahoma Christian's one and only sit-in, landing some of them in jail.

So, I was fortunate. The seeds that would cause me to question the status quo in almost every part of life, including that of women's role in the church, were sown early and well. The training and experience I received in thinking, reading and writing became the tools for my mild form of subversion.

I was fortunate, too, that in the storms to come about women's participation in the church, I had a trump card of sorts—I dislike doing anything public in church. I want only to sit and ruminate with no pressure to perform in any way. And, although I've spent the best years of my life doing lots of it, I'm not crazy about leading in the local congregation. As I once told my father, "I think I'm naturally lazy." To which he replied, "Everybody is naturally lazy."

Of course, so many women don't have such an easy out, and suffer from tremendous feelings of frustration, anger and angst about their exclusion from so many roles in their congregations.

But aside from having the tools to question and a lack of interest in public roles in the church, the how-to of using my gifts for the Lord while being a loving wife, mother, hostess, friend, daughter, sister, home renovator, interior designer, cook and nurse was uncharted territory. I started with a typical path: pursuing education in all its delights—both as a professor's wife and as a teacher myself.

A Supportive Husband

I married Ken Adams because I had never liked a man as much as I liked him, because he didn't seem threatened by me, and because Harold Fletcher told me he was a gifted musician with a great future.

Part Army kid and part Western Oklahoma boy, he embodied all that the more hidebound Tennessee men did not—he didn't have a host of restrictive expectations about women, he was adventurous, and he was an intellectual with an open mind. The fact that he turned out to be a gifted choral, orchestral and opera conductor, spending his career at Oklahoma Christian and taking me on more than two dozen performing tours, was icing on the cake.

As far as me and my hopes were concerned, he couldn't have been more supportive. I started my career as a high school English and journalism teacher—a career I chose because it was safe and predictable, yet rewarding and challenging. The thought of being a lawyer or doctor didn't occur to me—that was largely for the next generation of women. Instinctively I knew such a path, for me at least, would be too demanding to combine with having a family. And the ten years I taught high school and junior high before we had children were pleasant, easy and manageable.

Of course, all that changed with children.

With the birth of our first child, Elliott; of our second child, Meredith, who was severely handicapped; and our third child, Elizabeth, who was adopted, I devised a variety of plans to combine part-time or occasional full-time work with motherhood—all in work relating to journalism and public relations with Oklahoma Christian. I taught journalism classes at OC and sponsored the student newspaper; worked in public relations, designing and producing admissions and recruitment materials and producing the school catalog; and worked with the *Christian Chronicle*, which I now serve as assistant managing editor.

The reality of such work is that I and other women in part-time situations, both in church-related roles and otherwise, receive comparatively low pay, and often forfeit our status as "serious players"—in part because we don't have the emotional energy to jockey for position and visibility. We live with the reality that we are often more competent than men with full-time, better paying jobs. But all such choices are trade-offs, and the benefit for women is that part-time alternatives allow them to work in their fields and contribute to the family income, while making family life possible, and usually pleasant.

The Convergence of Change
But once again, my work at Oklahoma Christian has been under men I admire greatly—the late Bob D. Smith, a consummate thinker and strategizer; the fair-minded Lynn McMillon; the aforementioned Bailey McBride; and Scott LaMascus, a bright and gifted leader for now and the future.

So why am I going to such pains to relate the range of positive experiences I've had with men who were teachers or mentors or fellows in my experiences? Because I want to make clear that women's concerns about their opportunities in our fellowship are not necessarily based on hurt over mistreatment, on distrust or hatred of men, or on a history of conflict between the sexes—although, of course, such exists.

Concern about the role of women in the church is simply a matter whose time has come. Such concerns reflect a convergence of societal changes both in and out of our fellowship—an increase in the number of women entering professions, receiving post-graduate degrees, occupying leadership roles in government, education and industry. The higher educational level, generally, among our members fosters questioning of the givens in our fellowship and, consequently, greater openness in theology. And an increasing number of influential men believe women should no longer be second-class citizens in the church.

Yet the "backwards and in high heels" phenomenon affecting women gives rise to three central realities, one a general reality and two relating to the church. These are:

1. The reality that between the home and the market place, women are finding it hard to "do it all." Many are finding that doing everything is simply not possible, nor even wise.

15

For my generation a mentality existed that women should—in fact, must—"do it all" at one time. Our daughters' generation seems more prudent. Many young women today are deciding (as did some of their mothers) to live their lives in stages, alternating periods of full-time mothering with periods of full-time or part-time work while maintaining a home. Many are not trying to work two full-time jobs in order to show they can do it and be "real men." My generation has already established that.

Nonetheless, these women often reenter the work force to find themselves having lost ground in their fields and being behind on the latest developments and training. On the other hand, they have had the often marvelous experience of full-time parenting, which most men never have.

Men will not be the ones to develop good options for women wanting to combine mothering and a career. Women themselves will have to propose, hammer out, and outline alternative courses of action for their lives and careers, educating men to the demands they face. Such is true in and out of the church. With today's technology, the possibilities for part-time work at home, job sharing and alternate periods of part-time and full-time work are greater than they have ever been. Women must forge creative courses of action and convince men of their responsibility to be responsive to such plans.

2. The reality that in many Christian schools and ministries women occupy a majority of the support positions and few leadership positions.

The assumption that women in these institutions and ministries should serve in as limited a capacity as women are allowed to serve in the church must be questioned. That the vast majority of leadership roles in para-church agencies, in Christian colleges and universities and in Christian journalism are held by men should not be accepted as a given.

Expanding the longtime prohibition on women as preachers to exclude women from teaching roles in Bible and theology also must be reexamined. Often this is a comfort zone issue. Intellectually, many people—men and women, leaders and participants—know there is no rational reason to exclude women from such teaching roles. Excluding women is often a gut-level choice made because men are comfortable with the status quo in our institutions. Both men and women leaders should question such broad-based assumptions.

Irene Young Mattox, an outstanding leader in Churches of Christ in the middle of the last century, had to overcome the claim that a woman speaking on a lectureship program was akin to preaching. Mattox, the mother of today's leader Helen Mattox Young, stood her ground and paved the way for dozens of women to speak, lead classes and in other ways use their talents and abilities at church-related events.

Opportunities for women in the broader church community will expand in the future, but they will expand more quickly if old ways of thinking are routinely questioned.

Despite difficulties in combining the responsibilities of extended family life with the academic preparation needed for leadership roles and the challenge of full-time careers, many are able to achieve the balance. Such women must be given appropriate opportunities. Men must be convicted that, of all institutions in society, Christian institutions must be flexible and creative in helping women structure their careers to balance these demands and seriously consider women for leadership positions.

3. The reality of women whose opportunities in our congregations are limited to menial and support functions.

Sometimes women's options for service are limited because of repressive ideas about women generally or because of convictions about the scriptural range of activities women should participate in. However, it's often because of inertia—because it's always been that way, because women, or men, haven't wondered why. While the debate over women's role in public worship escalates, it must not be allowed to limit substantive leadership roles for women in the church.

A friend once told me she was given a list of ministries at her congregation and asked to choose ones to help with. As a woman, her options on the list came down to two—cooking for the sick and washing baptismal garments. As women in the church practice medicine and law, run businesses and fill a range of challenging roles in society, they will feel thwarted when their choices at church are limited and stereotypical.

Thoughtful observers in Churches of Christ know that women are and have been the backbone of local congregations—working behind the scenes, often in less than ennobling endeavors. Servanthood and service to home, family and community are central to the nature of many women in the church, particularly women of my generation and older. But the day is coming when our daughters and granddaughters will reject out of hand menial and mundane tasks in their fellowships, particularly if those are the only options for service they are given. Some will find creative ways to accomplish these tasks or pay someone else to do them.

The educational opportunities of women in the church—in Christian schools and otherwise—have come home to roost, and we must address the question of how these women will be able to use their abilities in our fellowship.

Accommodating Complexity

Today's women, although accomplishing much "backwards and in high heels," as my generation did, must not have to prove they are "real men" to have the opportunities they deserve, both in and out of the church. The realities of their complex lives must be accommodated. Most important, the debate over women's involvement in public worship must not be extrapolated to exclude women from roles of leadership in Christian colleges and universities, para-church ministries or local congregations.

I'm not saying women should be made elders tomorrow. Such a complex issue, with attendant references to scripture, will most likely be saved for future discussion. But aside from such issues—where all we are and believe in regard to hermeneutics and application of scripture must be brought to bear—universities, ministries and churches must believe and act in a way that honors the injunction "neither male nor female," and do so without delay.

I don't regret the many years I've lived out my life, my service, my ministry dancing "backwards and in high heels." Being a woman is a blessed role in life—only women give birth, usually only women have the option to combine family, careers and special interests. Only women have the opportunity to be friends of men in a way other men never can be.

I'm thankful that, as I've danced my dance, I've had the mentoring and approbation of Carroll Ellis, Harold Lipford, Harold Fletcher, Bob Smith and many others. That I wouldn't trade for anything.

If only someone had given me some—any—advice on how to "do it all," as the confluence of my times seemed to demand and afford.

Lindy Scobey Adams taught high school English and journalism for 10 years, and is now assistant managing editor for *The Christian Chronicle*—covering national news, special reports, and in-depth features.

Lindy and her husband Ken have two children: Elliott, a junior at Portland State University, and Elizabeth, a sixth grader. A daughter, Meredith, who was multiply handicapped, died in 1995 at age 11.

2

A Little Story about Jumping

Jackie Warmsley

Once upon a time, when my granddaughter, Ashley, was a toddler instead of the beautiful young woman she is now, she taught me a profound lesson, extending the boundaries of mind understanding to deep heart knowledge. She pounded actions into faith-words when faith gives pause to logic.

Ashley's daddy, my son, had called to ask if I would like to watch the girls swim at the "Y." My grandmotherly response was yes, and soon we were in the steamy pool area. I sat in the grandmother section responding appropriately to the yells of "Look!" "Look!" "Watch me!" "Watch me!"

Ashley's two older sisters were swimmers, taking turns jumping off the diving board, having pre-Olympic races and fearlessly attempting flips from time to time. Ashley was in the shallow end with her daddy, practicing putting her face under the water and blowing bubbles. She was delighted to see the beauty she could create.

Yet from time to time, Daddy would say, "Ashley, let's go to the deep end where you can jump off the diving board. Okay?" And Ashley would put her little hand into his big hand and walk with him to the deep end of the pool where he would slip into the water and she would bounce to the end of the diving board, squealing and yelling for all to pay attention. Then she would jump into his arms! He would take her to the safety of the side where the ritual would be repeated until he tired and suggested the shallow end and bubbles again.

I watched, fascinated. Never one time did I hear Ashley say "I can't swim" when the deep end was suggested. Never did I hear her fearfully suggest "But I might drown," or "My feet won't reach the bottom of the pool." She didn't even ask "Will you catch me?" No! In total trust, she just jumped! She knew her feet wouldn't touch the bottom. She knew she couldn't swim. What had her young mind learned? Why did she have no fear? She totally trusted her father, and she knew he would take care of her! She knew that, if she went into the deep end with him, there was nothing to fear! She was not alone!

My heart watched as my mind let the lesson soak in. That is exactly what God wants from me. Why do I argue when God suggests we go to the deep end? Why do I want to say I can't do it? Is it because I don't really trust him to take care of me? I have to do what Ashley did—take my father's hand and walk with him into the deep water. When he says, "Come," I must not be afraid to jump. He will catch me! I have to practice Jordan-River faith.

The truth was profound but simple. The application in action was soon to consume me, and many times I would be guided by the memory of a toddler holding her daddy's hand, bravely and confidently walking to the deep end of the pool and jumping into the water unafraid, because she trusted totally her father's arms.

Living in the 'Deep End'

I am a social worker by gift. I say this because it was what I was long before I knew what the words meant, before the term was applied to a certain career. I was a social worker before government plans and programs, when God's Word told churches to take care of widows and orphans and feed the poor and visit those in prison. I don't recall many sermons about these activities, because churches were abdicating their responsibility to a government that demeaned widows and orphans and barely kept the poor from starving and only knew how to build more and more prisons to shield "good people" from even seeing the cruel, ungodly treatment that went on inside the dark, demonic halls of punishment. After all, if we can succeed in branding our world "good," and the world of the unfortunate and disadvantaged "bad," we can stay apart rather than being part of the solution.

Jesus went to the people. Somehow, churches declared that if people were good, they would come to him. The government did a poor job of distributing services, because they worked without God's heart, and the churches abdicated more and more "deep end of the pool" works to the all-encompassing system.

This was the atmosphere I grew up in. Why would a person be drawn into such a whirlpool of confusion? Why should she desire a life's work of endless tasks in the scary deep end of the pool? Did I mention the word gift? Yes, gift! God instilled into my heart, even before it beat its first beat, the deep and awesome wonder of being able to actually feel what others felt. How could this be a gift, a present, when it caused pain and suffering, even tears, as I watched others struggle or heard the cry of neglected children or felt the prisoner's plea for understanding and mercy?

God gave me my gift so I could!

"Dear Lord! The water is too deep for one little girl to jump into. I will drown!"

"No! I will catch you! I will catch you every time!"

My gift was recognized for the first time by a fourth grade teacher. The children in her room sat in double desks where we twittered fourth grade secrets to each other when she wasn't looking. Passing notes was easy, too, and the world of problems was beyond our understanding. In the back of our room sat a boy, several years older than the others, who had severe learning problems. At that time, there were no special education classes, and the boy sat there, isolated by his handicap, not expected or expecting to take part. At recess, he stood and watched the others play. I don't recall being touched by his apparent loneliness, but my teacher decided to water the seed of my gift so it could grow. One day, my teacher asked me to stay after school, which I did. She asked if I would let Charles sit in the double desk with me so I could help him. She asked if I would try to include him in recess activities, and I said I would. This was deep water for a little girl, and I was not aware of God's help in the task, but I was curiously drawn to it. My teacher saw something in my personality that was open to this "calling," and the next day Charles was moved up front with me.

I remember how bad his tennis shoes smelled. He was dreadfully slow at learning what I so diligently tried to teach, but daily I tried. I would take him by the hand to include him in recess games, and I would choose him to be on my side in spelling bees, knowing he would cost points, because I was learning something more valuable than "readin', 'ritin' and 'rithmetic." I was learning how good it felt to see the smile on his face when he was chosen to be a part of the group, and I was learning how much fun it was to give without the anticipation of receiving.

I was also learning how important Charles really was. I liked him, and he liked me in return. Although I did not perceive it at the time, the wisdom of this teacher and the experience she put in motion changed my life and pointed it in the direction God had intended all along.

A gift! Thank you, God, for giving me the gift to recognize the tears behind the mask of another human being, for giving me the desire to do something about it, and for giving me the ultimate joy of your love when I do!

Practicing Obedience

What better gift could be given? God does not call the equipped, but he equips the called. He shapes each of us into the vessel he wants us to be—every detail, every talent given, is molded into the framework. All we have to do is take his hand, walk with him to the deep end of the pool, and jump! The more times we jump with him catching us, the more we know that he will. What a beautiful gift to be entrusted with, the treasure of what God loves the most—the people he created! And although our missions might be done in different ways, go different directions or along different paths, isn't that the gift he has given us all!

How awkward I was in practicing during the years that followed. How many were the lessons learned by failures resulting from my lack of faith and prideful meanderings. But I was being tutored by a patient God who rarely scolded as he molded me with his fatherly touch. He breathed love into me at every opportunity and never declared me "done" enough to turn me loose on my own. He wouldn't let me boss when I wanted to, and his disciplines were as kind as I would allow them to be. He knew he had me in the right field as he led me through working the streets, loving those labeled unlovable and walking through prison gates to teach and be taught. I learned to be less judgmental as I looked deeper into myself to measure the extent of what I had been given. I pondered God's Word more deeply as I studied his personality and the reasons for his callings. I progressed fearfully from the safety of the diving board to the ocean's stormy seas, and always the command was to jump, with the promise of his ability and faithfulness to catch me.

At times, fear gripped me, and like Peter, I began to sink. But as I practiced obedience, I became less fearful, because his part was always bigger than mine, and he always did his part. He told the Israelites to put their feet in the rushing waters of the Jordan before he parted the waves so they could walk across. Surely the priests walking ahead carrying the ark must have thought, "This ark is heavy, and if I put my feet in that swirling water, I'm going to go down!" But faith led them to obey, so God could manifest his mighty miracle for them!

Over and over I heard God tell me to put my feet in the water. *"Deliver groceries down that dark alley, Lord? I can't! I won't? I'll wait! I will! I will? I will!"* And never did God let the dark alley consume me when he had given me the command to go. He covered for me many times when I foolishly blundered ahead of him. He works that way, too.

So, for years, God led me in and out of places I had never dreamed of in my early sheltered life. Dark alleys became commonplace, and courtrooms and jails and prisons became avenues of God's call to reform. Social worker became my name and profession and academic preparation. But it was not as important as being what God wanted me to be. The name "Christian" was what I really was.

Church pews felt uncomfortable when so many seats were empty beside me. I felt more and more the tug of stormy seas that only the knowledge of Jesus Christ could calm, not only for me, but for the drug addict selling his soul for a mess of pottage, the alcoholic drowning in his own vomit and the prisoner seeking freedom when he or she had no idea of what freedom was or how it could be found. Why had so many churches looked away while the "undesirables" paraded en masse through the streets around them? Who deemed churches to be safe places instead of havens for those devoid of hope?

I made a sign which I put on my desk: "Ships are safe in harbor, but that is not what ships are made for!" The application was apparent to me. Christians might feel safe going to church three times a week, but that is not all Christians are made for.

"Jump!" the Father kept saying. *"Follow me to the deep end!"* God kept prodding me. *"The water is rough out here, but it's where the fish are,"* the Master Fisherman yelled over the noise of the storm.

I had to listen and obey to reap the benefits of his awesome miracles. How beautifully he has led me. How reassuring the touch of his hand as he leads me into deep waters. Why as human beings are we still reluctant to jump? It gets easier, and I am still learning. I ask God never to stop teaching me as I praise him for the wonderful blessings of the deep end, the stormy seas when he is there. He is there because he said he would be there, in the storm and in the promise of the rainbow that follows. My part is to believe and to act on my belief!

An 'Ocean-Storm Experience'

In February of 1992, I received a phone call from my son that was to begin an "ocean-storm experience" for me, although I did not know it at the time. It was just a simple, "Come over this evening to talk to us about something we've been thinking about." Sounded like a good evening, and always good food, because his wife Kit is an excellent cook and my willing and faithful prayer partner. This son, Bobby, is an emergency room doctor at a large local hospital who spends his time and money going to Ghana, West Africa, several times a year as a missionary, using his gift to heal souls as well as bodies. An evening with those two was always stimulating and exciting. The bonus? Three granddaughters to love and admire.

At the time, I was two-and-a-half years away from retiring from a Mental Health, Mental Retardation State facility. I was counting down the months until I could go barefoot as much as I wanted and see the telephone as a comfortable friend instead of a perpetual enemy. I had grown reasonably adept at jumping off the diving board into my Father's arms, and had grown to realize how strong they really were. I'd even experienced a few ocean-wave happenings. The streets and alleys were no longer scary to me, and jails and prisons were no longer a threat to my safety, but a joyful opportunity to uphold Jesus as Savior instead of a curse word used by angry men and women. I was 65 years old, and God had spent more than 40 years bringing me to this place and time—after wandering in the wilderness—while he whittled me, pounded me and kept me on the potter's wheel, even when I tried to jump off.

So I went, comfortably attired in sloppy sweats and unused running shoes. The three of us sat around the kitchen table drinking hot chocolate and eating homemade cookies while Bobby voiced his concern and we all offered our solutions.

The problem? Bobby had become increasingly concerned by seeing people, mostly men, on street corners with signs that read, "I'll work for food." He had seen the error of treating these homeless people professionally with medications and then sending them out into the bitter cold where their condition worsened instead of improved. The question, What could we do? turned into a vision which, on our part, was dreadfully small. The vision of God's thinking was large, as he enticed us into taking that first step into the Jordan River, that first jump into the deep end.

The answer, as we saw it, was that I would get a list of condemned houses from the City, and we would pick out one and use Bob's money to fix the plumbing and turn on the electricity and heat so people would have a place to be protected from the weather. I dutifully did my part, and armed with lists of addresses, spent several lunch hours and after-work hours looking at abandoned houses. I became increasingly aware of why the City had condemned them. It wasn't going to work. My social worker mind also started wondering about numbers and drugs and legal responsibilities for such an open house. Who would keep up the repairs?

I walked into one empty house with broken glass on the floor, a filthy mattress among the scatterings of sacks and cans and old newspapers used for coverings. Drug paraphernalia was everywhere, and in the midst of it all was a tattered, dirty teddy bear! The realization hit my heart with both fists. A baby, a child had been there. This was not a deep end of the pool problem, but a stormy ocean experience. Where were the churches while this child was witnessing hell's darkest door? Where was I?

Asking for Shelter

I kept passing by a large building that had once been a grocery store with a surrounding parking lot. It had been a junk place several times, but now it was boarded up. Trash blew around the door and a one-time fence in the back had blown over and was rotting. I was curious enough to peep through the cracks in the boards to see the large expanse of littered space inside, with one standing door that might lead to a bathroom. I was also curious enough to go through the courthouse records to find out who owned the property.

The property belonged to the J. C. Pace Co. in Fort Worth, Texas. I had no knowledge of these people, and they certainly had no knowledge of me, but I obtained a phone number, not even sure I would use it. Each day, I passed the property going to and from work. But the Spirit had planted the picture of a teddy bear in my heart, so one day I picked up the phone, dialed the number and asked to speak to Mr. Pace.

"Pertaining to what?" I was asked.

"Property in Abilene," I answered.

"I'll put you through to our real estate broker," I was told.

I realized I had more than a mom and pop organization on the line, and to the inquiry, "How can I help you?" I started asking questions, "How much floor space?" "Does the bathroom facility work?"

As I carefully took notes, something profound happened to me. A thought—not my thought—but spoken plainly to me by the Holy Spirit as he whispered, *"Ask if he will give you the building!"* My spirit pulled back as I argued silently, *"Lord! I can't do that! I don't mind asking for old tennis shoes or used clothes or dented cans of food, but I can't ask for a building."* I started talking faster and louder to the broker to drown out the noises in my head. I wanted to hang up fast. A pause came as I fumbled for a closing, and the Spirit said impatiently, "I said to ask him if he will give you the building!"

I took a deep breath and blurted out, "Would you consider giving this building to someone in Abilene who would like to make a shelter for homeless people?"

"Yes, we would!" he said. Then he modified the gift by saying, "We won't give it to an individual or to a church, but we will give it to a city." Stunned, I thanked him and said I would get back in touch. Tearfully, I thanked God and said I'd get back in touch with him, too.

The next few months repeatedly verified God's goodness and his faithfulness to finish what he starts. I literally could not run fast enough to keep up with his giving. I went before the City commissioners, and they voted to accept the property and to pursue funds to aid the adventure. I was led to an organization called "The Abilene Association of Congregations," made up of representatives of 23 different churches who were looking for a project and voted to back this one at my first presentation. A board of directors was appointed from this group—proven civic leaders with abilities far exceeding the normal.

What had started as a kitchen table idea now had a building worth $150,000 before repairs; the backing of a city and a workforce of 22 churches! In July of 1992 the city deeded the property to the Board of Directors of this program which now had a name, Hope Haven. As a result of a newspaper report of the birth of this dream, a woman in a nearby farming community sent a check for $100,000. She didn't know any of us, but she believed in what we were doing.

In September of 1992, I quit my job to devote full time to what I knew was being directed by God. I had a small savings, and I knew I could survive whatever lay ahead.

During the next three months, I traveled from North Texas to South, from Dallas to Houston, visiting 28 homeless shelters so I might have a pattern to follow in these uncharted seas. I saw multitudes of suffering people and many programs that, while beneficial, were putting band aids on cancer wounds, with masses of people going through revolving doors—in and out, in and out.

The Spirit was teaching me in these long hours on the road (as he talked and I listened) to formulate a program whereby Hope Haven would become a support system for homeless people who would commit themselves to being trained for jobs, staying off drugs and alcohol and submitting to counseling and the opportunity for spiritual guidance. An assembly of volunteers was organized—teachers from Abilene's three universities to teach; doctors and nurses to provide medical care; dentists to repair neglected teeth; counselors to give one-on-one counseling, an organization to provide glasses, pharmacists to collect medication samples, and spiritual leaders to give guidance.

Opening the Doors

In June of 1993, Hope Haven opened its doors to its first recipient—a young mother and her two-year-old daughter who had been born in a vacant warehouse. The mother had been "on the streets" since the age of 13, but was now tired of drugs and insecurity and wanted a better life for her daughter.

Others soon followed into the newly built facility, designed by volunteer contractors with a volunteer architect's touch into a beautiful place with a dormitory room for eight single men, a dormitory room for eight single women and four family living quarters. Family was defined as having children, even if the parent were single. An abundance of food came in from a loving community, to the extent that we had food to give away. Around-the-clock supervision was provided by a paid staff as we were given the opportunity to defuse myths surrounding those who struggle against odds that we, who are more fortunate, cannot begin to comprehend.

We became a struggling but loving community. All ages survived in this small survival area. Grandpas babysat with the babies (one born there). People who had not known trust became "sisters" and "brothers," transcending age, background and race. We helped each other, and tutors were obtained when lessons were too difficult or someone just wanted to learn to read. The mentally disadvantaged were sheltered instead of being preyed on by others. I learned more than anyone. I never did so many jobs I didn't know how to do.

All residents with the ability to do so were required to get their GED, and the Adult Education program services provided more than an education. Sunday School classes took up collections for books and supplies. The first year we were in operation, four residents went on, after obtaining their GED's, to enroll in college with federal grant money! A job consultant for company seminars volunteered to teach a night a week on job interviews and resume writing. There were even style shows on proper dress. So many clothes came in that we shared with other agencies. High school youth groups built a new fence—paying $50 a section to put it up. In one day, 350 kids swarmed like ants performing the job under the supervision of a professional fence company, while Coca Cola donated drinks and hot dogs, which were served by the residents.

Did it work? It works for those who want it to work for them. But it provided a service beyond what it gave the residents. Hope Haven provided a place, a safe place, for those who wanted to give. Cookies from a ladies' Bible class; playground equipment and an outside barbecue shelter from the Junior League; computers and washing machines and a contest between our two high schools to see who could collect the most paper goods, which resulted in pick-up truckloads of toilet paper that led to the gift of a storage building. A second grade Sunday School class had a car wash to try to raise $200 for a projector and quit at 1:30 with $600 to gleefully give. We all learned more about miracles, and who can put a price tag on that?

I resigned my job as executive director in September of 1996. I was seventy years old, and God had whispered kindly that it was time for younger minds and bodies to challenge the 10- to 12-hour days that never stopped. I had seen so many miracles, watched so many people change their lives completely, grieved to the pit of my soul when some made bad choices, seen the lost give their lives to Jesus. My faith was restored so many times that even ocean waves didn't scare me, so long as I kept my eyes on Jesus and my hand in God's hand. Jumping off the diving board seemed easy, even though I still couldn't swim by myself.

Do I thank God? Every day, for countless blessings. I thank him that he has led me through storms and choppy seas to the time in my life when I can read more, paint some and go barefoot a lot. I rejoice when I receive phone calls from past residents saying, "I still have a job," or "God has kept me sober," or just "Thank you." I now can better follow God's admonition to "Be still and know that I am God!" I am grateful!

Hope Haven? By the year 2000, over 500 people have lived through its experiences. I believe that all have benefited, even those whom more judgmental people might call failures. I see them as strugglers, as seed not yet sprouted which, with help, might become the most beautiful flowers of all. Hope Haven is now in the process of opening a second donated building, so more might be helped. I am grateful for that, too.

But most of all, I am grateful to God for letting me be a part of all this, that I might better know how willing he is to work patiently and lovingly with people like me.

Jackie Morris Warmsley holds the B.S. in social work from Abilene Christian University. She was a caseworker with Christian Service Center, a school counselor with The Bridge, director of Teen Development, Inc., a social worker at Abilene State School, and executive director of Hope Haven Shelter for the Homeless. She has also served as a counselor at Taylor County Jail and the Texas Department of Corrections.

Jackie served on the Mayor's Committee on Minority Relations and Community Problems, on the Abilene Housing Authority Board, as a member of Governor Mark White's Citizen's Committee studying prison problems, and on the board of directors of Big Brothers/Big Sisters.

She is married to Ray L. Warmsley and has three children and six grandchildren.

3

Opening Doors:
The Journal of a Minister

Katie Hays

Sunday school; Tahoka (Texas)
Church of Christ; 1980-something
(I'm not sure about the year, but we had to be older than twelve. I know this because Dad was the teacher, not Mom.)

Dad says, "So my question is, why one verse and not the next? or the previous? How do we make distinctions in God's word line by line? First Timothy 2:11 says 'Let a woman learn in silence with full submission.' And just a few verses up from that, 'In every place the men should lift their holy hands in prayer.' Well, I'm asking, which part have we got wrong? Which is it? Should we be lifting our hands when we pray? Or do women no longer have to learn in silence?"

My memory stops with the asking of the question. It's probably safe to guess that there were no sufficient answers offered that morning, or in any such Sunday school class for a long time to come. The two or three students in class were just kids; my dad was giving voice to the first significant spiritual struggle he'd ever confessed, at least to me. But for me, it was the question that made the difference. It was the question that opened the door.

**Sunday afternoon; Harvard University
graduate school housing, 1987**

She comes into the world's smallest kitchen with another load of dirty dishes from the table and puts them in the sink where I am washing. It's her apartment, hers and her husband's, and I am enchanted by it. I would wash dishes all night just to stay here, near her, near them.

They are both in graduate school studying the things of God; that's all I understand about their degree programs. His will prepare him for more study, maybe a Ph.D; hers will lead to (gasp!) ministry. In a (gasp!) church. She wants to preach. She does, in fact, preach. At the Church of Christ where I worship. They sometimes give me a ride there, in their VW Beetle with the plastic Hawaiian leis around the stick shift. Sometimes she drives; sometimes he does. How slowly can I wash these dishes? How long will they let me stay?

Partly, of course, I want to stay because my own school life is coming apart. In the second year of my engineering course work at M.I.T., I am coming apart at the seams. The schoolwork means nothing to me. The social scene is eating me up. The goals of my classmates are not my goals; their ways are not my ways. I have chosen engineering because in the '80s, even in small-town Texas, we know that women can do anything in the world. In the world, not in the church. Here in this Harvard apartment, with the world's smallest kitchen, I am learning another way. I'm pretty sure it is a better way. The dishes all cleared, she joins me at the sink to rinse and dry. Don't help, I think. Let me do this, at least. This one thing I know how to do. But she's more of a talker than a dishwasher, anyway. So she talks, and I strain to commit each word to memory.

"I think you will not be an engineer," she says. "Sometimes someone has to tell you the truth. I don't think it's for you. Someone told me, when I was standing at a kitchen sink doing dishes just like you are now, that what I had picked was not the right choice. Someone told me it would be ministry, it would be preaching. I'm telling you, Katie-bug, I think it will be preaching for you, too."

She calls me Katie-bug because I told her once that my mother calls me that, and she thinks it's cute. It usually annoys me, but this

afternoon it is the least of my problems. This preaching thing again—
it's not the first time she's brought it up. It won't be the last. It's as if
she found the door in my heart barely ajar and has stuck a crowbar
in to pry it all the way open, inch by inch. Thank goodness she's so
skinny. I'm pretty sure it will take a long time.

One full year, Abilene Christian University, 1988-89
It didn't take as long as I thought. On leave of absence now from
M.I.T., I have carried the map of the better way I learned in the col-
orful, convoluted streets of Cambridge and Brookline to the pale, flat
grid of Abilene. Maybe this map won't get me anywhere here, though.
Maybe I've reached a dead end.

As soon as I got there in the fall, someone must have scratched my
name onto a campus bathroom stall: "For a good argument, call Katie
at 676-xxxx." I have to study harder, smarter, longer than my classmates in the Bible Department, because the burden of proof is on me
in every class, every conversation. I am learning both sides of the
"women's role" debate, committing every exegetical detail to memory.
Sometimes my opponents don't know their own arguments, which
makes it awfully hard to argue with them.

Then, the spring: resurrection, even in Abilene. Dr. F—opens the
socio-historical world to me; pushes David Balch's dissertation[1] into my
hands. "You'll need this," he says. Dr. G—opens the Greek text in class
but shares his Boston University papers on gender in the New
Testament behind closed office doors. Dr. R—opens his preaching
course to all who register, no strings attached. It's almost enough to
make me forget the ones who close their doors in my face; the tuition
bills I can't pay and can't get a scholarship for; the lady who chases me
to chapel every day so she can lay hands on me and pray—in front of
God and everyone!—that I will be forgiven "for wanting to be a man."

Oh, did I mention? There's a boy in Abilene, soon to be a man,
who knows his arguments, his Greek, himself. A boy, soon to be a
man, who wants to know me, too. I decide against returning to Cambridge. There are places in Texas to be explored.

An autumn Sunday afternoon; New Haven, Connecticut; 1993

Having sojourned in Texas for three years, finally cobbling together his-n-her degrees in Bible from the Institute for Christian Studies in Austin, we are once again in the northeast. "Once again" for me, anyway. It's his first time, this Texan husband who cooks because I do the budget. Life is easier for me here. No one calls me "sweetheart" in the grocery store or the gas station. Enrollment at the divinity school is about even, gender-wise. Nobody much cares whether I preach or not.

Except at church. The "div school boys" take turns in the pulpit, drawing $75 a pop for sermons recycled from preaching classes and doctoral seminars. I'm allowed an active role in the church, too, building a campus ministry to Yale students and teaching every Bible study they'll let me teach. But no salary, no turn in the pulpit. It's a church living on the sickening edge of the gender justice cliff, tipping drunkenly back and forth, making everybody inside woozy with waiting.

"Woozy" is a mild word for how I feel. "Vertigo" is the name of the symptom for which the student health clinic can give me no diagnosis, no prognosis, no cure. I simply cannot stand up straight or walk a straight line. Nausea and dizziness make me cling to the hallway walls when I have to be out. At home I stay in bed. Reading is impossible. It's worse on Sundays.

On this particular Sunday afternoon, we are in a job interview. Lance and I have, against good advice we now wish we'd heeded, applied to share the full-time ministry position at this congregation upon our graduation in the spring. The job was not advertised as being open for women. But maybe, we're thinking, it's time for all of us to jump off this cliff together. The church is not convinced. This afternoon, the church has gathered in a member's living room, ostensibly to ask questions of us, whom they have known for almost three years. Here's one exchange from that interview:

Church member to female interviewee: "This church is not strong. It will die if it gets any weaker. Do you know what will make this church weak? Do you?"

Female interviewee: mouth opening and closing like a fish, unable to formulate an answer.

Church member: gesturing with her finger, leaning toward female interviewee, "You. You will. You will make this church weak."

The door slams shut. A friend mails me a card with a Far Side cartoon on the front: two deer talking in the forest, one with a red and white bulls-eye on his chest. The other deer says to him, "Bummer of a birthmark, Hal." The vertigo rages on.

A few weeks later, another Sunday afternoon; New Haven; 1993
The phone rings. Lance will have to answer it; I am in bed trying to will the ceiling to stop spinning. I hear him murmuring "uh-huh, uh-huh," then interrupting his caller. "Sir, I just want to make sure you understand. You know that my wife and I both want to be ministers? Not just me?" He says this about every thirty seconds into the phone. I don't know what his silent, invisible conversation partner is saying; only that Lance keeps interrupting him. "Sir, excuse me for saying this again, but I just want to be as clear as I can. My wife and I both are graduating this spring. We're both looking for jobs in ministry. —Uh-huh. —Uh-huh. Okay. I'll tell her. Bye."

The door is wide open now. The silent, invisible caller is, in fact, an elder from the Cahaba Valley Church of Christ in Birmingham, Alabama. ("Where?" I will ask and be asked a million times over the next few months.) He has our resumes and our letter explaining that we will share a job, any job, in any Church of Christ where women can participate in work and worship. They have such a job to offer. He wants us to come to Birmingham for an interview.

The door is wide open now, and cannot be closed. Though some will try.

A good four-and-a-half years later; Shelby County, Alabama; 1994-1999
Alabama is a funny place to live, at least for me, at least for now. The guy at the Citgo station on the corner calls me "Miss America" and "sweetheart" and looks at me everywhere but in the eye. But at church, in my office, on Sundays, during worship, in elders' meetings, Galatians 3:28 is coming true. It's a welcome reversal from the Connecticut situation. My "bummer of a birthmark" is fading, almost invisible.

Almost—story of my life.

One day a woman from church invites me to lunch, tells me she can't be at our church anymore because I disappoint her; she thought with the addition of a woman to the ministry staff, things would be better, more equitable, more something. She hoped her concerns would be better represented now that there was a woman in the elders' meetings. I'm overwhelmed by her need for me to represent All Women, be Every Woman. Does she know how differently other women in the church would ask me to represent them in elders' meetings? The Whitney Houston song, "I'm Every Woman," a pop hit on the radio a few years back, keeps running through my head. I always hated that song; now it makes my bulls-eye birthmark flare up again.

Another day, a Sunday between class (which I have taught) and worship (in which I am preaching), a woman stops me in the hallway. She tells me she can't be at our church anymore after many years because of family pressure. "As long as we just talked about it, it was one thing. Now you're here, I can't be. I'll be looking for another church, and it's because of you." Just like that. Knocks the breath out of me without touching me. I feel the bulls-eye birthmark brightening. Another day, another woman, an invitation to chat at her house. The conversation eventually comes to this: the politics of gender and power in church, or to be more specific, our church. "I'll put it this way," she says. "When you come into the church kitchen to say hello to the women who have gathered around the coffee pot on Sunday mornings, everybody's nice. When you leave, it's another story. You never want to be the first one to leave that kitchen on Sunday mornings."

"You mean 'you,' like 'One never wants to be the first one?'" I ask. "Or you mean me?"

"You," she says. She looks happy to have made me squirm.

Ministry is a conspicuous job. We say it's about humble servanthood; we say we serve a priesthood of believers; I am but one of many who are called to the ministry of reconciliation Paul talks about in 2 Corinthians 5. But a certain amount of this kind of ministry is done in front of the church, and when you invite people to look at you for a little while each week they don't stop because you step down from the pulpit. When you wear a bright red-and-white bulls-eye on your chest, i.e., when you are a woman—the first woman (so people think no matter how much Restoration history you bring up), the only woman (so people think and are probably right, for now anyway), and not the perfect woman by a longshot—they look at you all the more.

Ministry is a conspicuous job. A woman in ministry in a Church of Christ has perhaps the most conspicuous job in the world. At least in our small world. When the door is wide open, people feel free to look right in. What can you say? You invited them to take their best shot. Don't be surprised when they do.

The same four-and-a-half years in Alabama, however, produce more lessons than one. For instance, there are more people than just me for whom doors are opening, who are experiencing the wonder of looking out and the vulnerability of being seen.

. . . Like the seventy-something man who had not been convinced by Bible study that women should teach and preach, but who demonstrated an unfailing commitment to unity in the church family he loves. He sacrificed his personal comfort in more ways than one to attend the first adult Sunday school class I taught, climbing the stairs to a stuffy second-floor room every week for an entire quarter to listen, learn and argue. He honored me with his arguments: he didn't want to argue about me, just the text and the often naive interpretations of a brand-new, fresh-out-of-school teacher. He complained about one of my sermons to the elders because of something I said, but not because I said it. In the moment, he drove me crazy. With time, I learned to thank God that, when he and I flung open our respective doors and looked out, we found ourselves eye to eye.

. . . Like the elder who carried a rocking chair into the back of the auditorium every Sunday morning so I could breastfeed my newborn on either side of a sermon. The day I preached, heard a confession of Jesus' lordship from a teenager I'd been studying with, wrestled with a stuck skirt zipper trying to get into clothes suitable for baptizing, ended up with a wet skirt anyway, and scurried to the back to receive a hungry baby while communion was being passed, this humble man laid towels in the seat of the rocking chair and around my shoulders,

41

then gave us our privacy till the trays came around. If Jesus' disciples had been nursing moms who endured a rainstorm on their way to the upper room, our Lord would have done the same. Drying off instead of footwashing; bread and wine shared around the needs of an infant; doors opened to expose new categories of service. When ours opened to each other, my elder saw needs in me I didn't anticipate having; I saw gifts in him he didn't anticipate giving.

**Present day; Long Island, New York; for as long as
it seems good to the Holy Spirit and to us (Acts 15:28)**
Another church family with a wide open door, many members of which are blissfully unaware that the door ever was closed (because they have other backgrounds than Churches of Christ), has welcomed us home. Coming home: that's what it feels like every time a church says, "Come, live with us and break bread with us and share your best gifts with us." I live a life built on that gracious invitation and built up by the lessons offered gently and not-so-gently by those who push, pry, pull and otherwise contend with the doors God has opened in his people, his church. I have offered my story through disjointed narratives. Let me now make some observations based on living those stories.

The first observation is the most obvious and painful to admit: the door-closing Christians in these highly selective anecdotes have usually been women, and the door-opening saints have almost exclusively been men. I didn't choose the stories by those criteria; if I'd thought to make a list before I wrote, I would have employed a little affirmative action to avoid telling this particular truth.

Certainly, there have been women in my life who have supported, prayed for and given their assent to my ministry—and the ministry of all women who are so gifted. My own mother planted an obsession with the things of God in my heart, and the woman at Harvard showed me how to turn that obsession into a life of proclaiming God's good news to God's beloved people. Over the years, I have registered every kind of reaction from women who learn what I do for a living, from joyful disbelief to righteous indignation. Perhaps because I assumed that every woman would hear the message of gender justice as good news,

I have been more deeply affected by those who don't. And certainly there have been men along the way who have belittled, condemned and refused to allow my ministry—and the ministry of all women who are so gifted. Over the years, I have registered every kind of reaction from men who learn what I do for a living, from joyful disbelief to righteous indignation. Perhaps because I assumed that every man would hear the message of gender justice as bad news, I have been more deeply affected by those who heard it and responded to it as gospel.

Concerning women for whom this sounds like bad news: I have learned not to underestimate the hurt the question of gender roles can stir up, for them and for me. It hurts them in part, I think, because my presence in the pulpit or behind the Lord's table or at the podium carries an implied criticism of the work they have done so diligently for so long. Is not keeping the nursery week in and week out a worthwhile ministry? Visiting shut-ins, taking casseroles to funerals, tending to the details of births and baptisms, illnesses and deaths—most or all of the actual pastoral care that happens in congregational life—were these not enough to offer the church if in our "real" lives we were talented enough to manage households, classrooms, consulting firms, banks, government agencies and more? If we condemn the church for stifling the Spirit-gifts of women, are we also condemning the women who conceded to the system, led singing from their seats, turned "elder's wife" into an unofficial but powerful leadership role, and found exhausted contentment in the vast array of women's work required by a church family?

The lesson for women in ever-expanding ministerial roles, then, is something like this: when you are the beneficiary of a Spirit-led sea change and doors begin to open for you, some of the people you find staring back at you will think you took aim at them. They think they are wearing the bull's eye! The possibilities for hurt on both sides are great. Don't be afraid to employ the virtues for which women have traditionally been known: be gentle, humble, submissive and wise. Don't be afraid to employ the virtues which have often been seen as men's special gifts: be truthful, courageous, diligent and smart. Be exactly who God called you to be: his child, his servant.

The lesson for men for whom gender justice sounds like good news is that the discussion cannot only be about "the women's role in the church." Gender justice is about their own roles in the church, at home and in the world; the doors have been flung open to reveal a need for men to re-examine their own gifts and the service to which they might be called. In a church that doesn't make assumptions about who can preach based on gender, but rather discerns the gift of proclamation in whomever the Spirit has chosen, what might happen when the cradle-roll class needs a teacher or the Vacation Bible School needs a cookie volunteer for Thursday morning? The answer depends on whether the men of the congregation have grown into the fullness of their humanity along with the women whose knees shake when they read scripture in front of an assembly for the first time.

The lesson, then, for churches moving toward gender justice in the work, worship and leadership of the congregation is this: it is not enough—or is it too much?—to open new areas of service for women without challenging men to reassess their own lives of service in the kingdom. I long for a time when the reassessing and reevaluating are finished and we no longer have to remind men that they are eligible to sign up on the nursery duty clipboard. But churches have work to do in this area. The person who stands over the Lord's Supper and quotes 1 Corinthians 11, blessing and breaking the bread in the tradition of our humble messiah, should receive no more honor than the person who comes to church early to squirt grape juice into the little cups or the one who stays late to shake crumbs out of the plates and decide whether the paper doilies will last another week. Who, in this scenario, is the servant of all, the one promised greatness in the kingdom of God (Mk. 9:35)? The answer is complicated, for when the speaker, the preparer, and the dishwasher offer humble service according to their gifts and no other criteria, it will be hard to tell.

My second observation is that the ministry of reconciliation to which I am called (1 Cor. 5:17 ff.) has sometimes been rendered ineffective because my gender provokes conflict.

Here's how I think about the specific message I'm called to proclaim. The good news Christians have to share is that broken relationships can be healed because of God's amazing grace. He has poured out grace to close the rift between himself and his beloved creation. That same grace overflows in our lives so we can love our fellow human beings in the selfless tradition of Jesus of Nazareth. When we are filled with Jesus' Spirit, walls come down, anger and resentment drain away, enemies are reconciled, strangers become neighbors, doors are opened. A minister of reconciliation shapes that vocabulary into good news—the best news!—for a disconnected, alienated, bitterly individualistic society.

There has been enough conflict in my short life to last a long time, and I long now to follow Paul's exhortation in this life of ministry: "If it is possible, insofar as it depends on you, live peaceably with all" (Rom. 12:18). So far, God has opened doors that lead to places where it is (mostly) possible to be "just a minister" rather than a woman minister, or a women's minister, or anything other than the minister of reconciliation I believe he's called me to be. For the most part, present-day conflict about my vocation has come from strangers rather than members of the congregation I serve: vacationing visitors who get more than they bargained for when they found us in the Yellow Pages; individuals calling the church office to confirm rumors they've heard through "brotherhood" papers; or the entire Southern Baptist Convention, as represented on Larry King Live, after their recent decision to rein in their most gifted women.

What happens, however, when the minister-messenger, by her very presence, stirs up conflict, fear, embarrassment or resentment in individual members of the congregation to which she is called to serve up a good helping of reconciliation? It does happen. I can announce my intentions from sea to shining sea: "Peace to you who are far off! Peace to you who are near!" (Eph. 2:17). But I have to concede that walking around with this big bull's eye on my chest makes it look to some like I'd rather fight than reconcile! The "peace" proclamation from my mouth might sound like a challenge rather than a comfort.

What is the lesson, then, as I can change neither my gender nor my calling? Over time I have learned not to seek conflict, and not to be surprised when it comes despite my best efforts. Indeed, I have sometimes borne criticism from those who would like to hear me speak out for gender justice in all the churches, rather than rest comfortably in congregations where the battles were fought before I arrived. From those critics I have learned that to preach reconciliation on Sunday morning may mean I have to engage in a gender-justice skirmish on Monday afternoon. It may be with a stranger or a member of my congregation, but it should always be for the sake of being true to my calling and for the goal of opening doors a little wider for women and men who are peeking through the cracks, waiting to see what's possible in the upside-down world of God's kingdom.

Most of all, I have learned to be grateful toward those wise and generous women and men who risked their fingers and feet and necks to keep the door from slamming shut on me. What can I do but risk the same to keep open the doors that God unlocks for his daughters and sons every day? This, too, is the ministry of reconciliation, the bringing together of women and men, women and women, women and their gifts, women and their churches. The doors are heavy; the targets painted on all our chests are large and frighteningly visible. But God calls us to this work, this ministry of reconciliation. I've never yet seen him assign a task he didn't give us the gifts to do!

Just one more story: Some years ago a man in the Cahaba Valley Church in Birmingham was stopped in the grocery store by a fellow from another Church of Christ in town who wanted to confirm the rumors he'd heard. "Is it true," he asked, "that women served communion in your church last Sunday?" "Hmm...," replied the Cahaba Valley member, "you know, I don't remember." That is gender justice. May it come soon for us all.

Note

1. David L. Balch, *'Let Wives Be Submissive': The Origin, Form, and Apologetic Function of the Household Duty Code (Haustafel) in 1 Peter* (Yale University, 1974).

Katie Hays and her husband of ten years, Lance Pape, are co-ministers at the West Islip Church of Christ in New York. They share one full-time job so each can stay home with their two young children, Lydia and Jack. Katie and Lance alternate days "on the job," so responsibilities from preaching to taking out the garbage are shared.

Katie grew up in West Texas. She attended MIT and ACU before graduating from the Institute for Christian Studies in 1990. After receiving a Master of Library and Information Science degree at the University of Texas, she went to Yale Divinity School, where she and her husband earned M.Div. degree in 1994. She and Lance previously ministered together at the Cahaba Valley Church of Christ in Birmingham, Alabama.

4

For Everything
There Is a Season

Joyce Hardin

The story of my spiritual journey has to begin with a walk when I was in the third grade in Abilene, Texas. My mother would dress me and my two younger sisters in our Sunday best and send us off to the Church of Christ several blocks down the road where we would attend Sunday school and worship and then walk home again. It was my responsibility to make sure my sisters behaved and were well cared for, and I took that responsibility seriously. Occasionally, one elder would drive us home, and I remember his taking me aside after one such drive and telling me how important it was that I continue to come to church and make sure that my sisters did as well. He said he knew it would not always be easy, but God would take care of me if I put my trust in him. I think that was the point when I truly began to believe.

My mother's family has a long history in Churches of Christ, dating back to the time of Alexander Campbell. At least one of her uncles was a preacher, and she was raised in a very strict Christian environment. Members of my father's family were anything but church goers! It has always amazed me that my mother and one of her sisters married brothers from this family which was so unlike their own. Both husbands were baptized, but not until much later. In my growing-up years, there was never a time that my family attended church together. I do not think my father prevented Mother from going, she just did not go without him. It was not until I was in college that assembling for worship became regular for my parents.

Though she did not go herself, Mother made sure that her daughters attended church wherever we lived—and we moved almost every year when I was in elementary and junior high school. She was an avid Bible reader, though, and often used scripture in teaching us lessons about life. She made sure that we knew the doctrine of the Church of Christ. My fondest memory of my mother is of gathering with my sisters around her chair and singing hymns. Her favorite was "What a Friend We Have in Jesus."

We moved to Artesia, New Mexico, when I was in the eighth grade, and it was there I decided it was time to be baptized. For the first time, my mother went to church and walked down the aisle with me. I never doubted that I knew what I was doing, and I was shaking from excitement as I went down into the baptistry. The woman who was helping me thought I was shaking from the cold, and she assured me that the water would be warm. She seemed not to realize that this was the most important moment of my life. I felt like a new person, and I thought everyone should be able to see me in a new way. It was disappointing that to others it was an ordinary Sunday afternoon. I remember that experience when I witness a baptism, and I pray that the church family of the new Christian will recognize, share and celebrate the birth of a new member of God's family.

I was always a good student, and I was determined to go to college. My mother encouraged me even though she could not imagine that it would be possible. My father felt that a college education would be wasted on a girl who would just get married and raise a family. I focused my hopes on a special scholarship that would pay all expenses to a state university. Only three from our school were allowed to apply and since I was one, I prayed hard that God would let me be the winner.

Hooked on Teaching

I cannot remember when prayer was not a part of my life. However, I often fell asleep before I closed with "in Jesus' name" and was not too sure those prayers counted. Mostly the prayers consisted of asking for God's help—whether it was to do well on a test or to get a good summer job or to receive a coveted award. It seemed that those prayers were almost always answered in a positive way, and I felt that God truly listened to me. However, when the scholarship that I so desperately wanted went to someone else, I was devastated and could not believe God had failed to answer this prayer which seemed so crucial to the rest of my life.

A few days after the scholarship was awarded, my father came home and announced that the preacher (whom he did not know and I knew only as a face in the pulpit) had visited him at work and told him that I needed to go to Abilene Christian College. Then he added that the next day, the three of us (my father, the preacher and I) would drive to Abilene to see about my enrolling there. I was completely taken by surprise. I had always wanted to go to a Christian college but had never mentioned it to anyone since it seemed impossible. About midway into my freshman year at Abilene Christian, I realized that if I had won that scholarship, I would not have been there. It was the first time I really thought about God's having a plan for my life. The phrase I had often uttered, "if it be Your will" took on an entirely new significance.

The first time someone told me I was going to be a teacher, I was in the fifth grade and I had never been so insulted in my life. I did not know exactly what I would be when I grew up but certainly something more exciting than a teacher. It was my high school principal who made the difference. He called me into his office one day and said he was starting a future teachers club and wanted me to help him. When I replied that I was not going to be a teacher, he just smiled and said, "Yes, you are—you just don't know it yet." He made me an unofficial substitute teacher, and during my senior year, I spent at least one day a week substituting in an elementary or junior high classroom. One of those experiences was in a segregated Black school in conditions that were appalling. The following Saturday, I walked past one of the young Black girls who had been in my class and heard her whisper to her mother, "That's my teacher." I was hooked! I not only wanted to be a teacher, but I wanted to make a difference in the lives of my students.

For me, the teaching profession has been very rewarding, but it has also carried a tremendous responsibility. I am often reminded of James 3:1 which admonishes, "Let not many of you become teachers for they shall incur a greater judgment." I have often wished that I could tell that high school principal just how much he affected my life. I am sure that he would smile if he knew how many times in my career as a teacher and a teacher educator that I have said to a searching and, sometimes struggling, individual, "You are going to be a teacher, you just don't know it yet!"

The years at Abilene Christian were a time of growing and maturing. I believe a Christian university should model itself after the statement made about Jesus in Luke 3:52, that he grew in wisdom and in stature and in favor with God and man. Not only was I trained for a profession, but the Bible classes, devotions, and chapel placed God at the center of my life. The Christian examples I found in my professors still affect me today. And, for the first time, I began to consider what I might be able to do in God's kingdom.

Marriage and Family

Like all girls of my generation, I hoped to get married and have a family. Even though my prayers always included a request that God send me someone to love who would love me in return, I was not at all sure it would happen. Most boys did not like girls with brains and, unlike some of my friends, I refused to play dumb. Then, there was the question of being in subjection—a common topic in the girls' dorm. I was strong-willed and decided that it might be better not to marry than to deal with the issue. I had been married for several years before I realized that there is more to Ephesians 5 than just verse 24 which says that wives should be subject to their husbands in everything as the church is to Christ. The answer comes in verse 25 where husbands are told to love their wives as Christ loved the church and gave himself up for her. When a husband loves his wife enough to die for her, then subjection presents no problem.

In the summer between my junior and senior years, my family moved to Albuquerque, New Mexico. Only the year before they had moved from Artesia to Carlsbad, and to me this indicated that the moves I disliked so much in childhood were beginning again. I told my father that I would not move again. However, as an unemployed and very broke college student, I had no choice but to go with the family—complaining, as my mother said, all the way. Our first Sunday in Albuquerque, our family went to church together, and two very significant events took place. My father, to the surprise of us all, was baptized, and I met a young man named Dan Hardin. If I had had my way, neither would have taken place. I try to think of that particular day whenever I find myself feeling confident that what I want is what God wants for me.

It would have been difficult to be a student at Abilene Christian in the fifties and not have some thought of doing mission work. Since I thought I would be an old maid school teacher, my plans were to teach for a few years in the States and then go overseas to some hardship area such as London or Paris or Switzerland. My first date with Dan changed that. We had hardly gone a block from my house when Dan told me that he planned to be a missionary in Seoul, Korea. Although he did not say it in so many words, I got the distinct impression that if I were not interested in the same thing, he might just take me straight back home, and I wanted to see the movie. That date resulted in a more than a 40-year involvement in missions, 17 of them in Korea.

Seasons of Life and Ministry

Solomon tells us that there is "a time for every purpose under heaven" (Eccles. 3:1). That sums up my life and perhaps my feminist philosophy as well. I did not necessarily plan it that way, but there are definite seasons in my life and in my ministry. There is some overlapping, of course, and one season often blends with another, but it has led me to say to young women, "You can have it all but not necessarily all at the same time."

For me, the gravity that held the seasons together has been my marriage. I firmly believe that commitment to my mate takes second place only to commitment to God. I have been blessed with a husband whom I not only love but who loves me enough to die for me. He has always encouraged me to be all I could be and has provided the support and care I needed during the storms and the calm that seasons inevitably bring into our lives.

I arrived in Korea in 1958 three months pregnant. When Mara was nine months old, we adopted Danna, a ten-day-old Korean baby, and nine months later, Terra, our third little girl, was born. With three babies under the age of two, I was a full-time mother. There were many pressures on me to teach and do other activities outside the home, but I felt God had given me the responsibility of raising my girls, and I could not give that task to anyone else.

As a educator, I am deeply concerned with the trend that encourages mothers to leave their small children with alternative "caregivers" in order to pursue a career. I recognize that in some situations there are no options. More often, I fear, the choice is made on the basis of either self-fulfillment or financial gain. Over the years, I have trained hundreds of young women to be professional educators. I have told each of them (and my own daughters) that my prayer has been that when they had young children, they would make it their profession to be a full-time mother. Careers can be put on hold, but children cannot. Training up a child in the way he should go so that when he is old, he will not depart from it (Prov. 22:6) is a parental responsibility, not that of a caregiver or even a Christian school. Fortunately, child rearing years are relatively short. When children reach school age, different decisions can be made, bearing in mind that parenting is one season that never completely goes away.

When my girls started to school, I was content to relax and enjoy my free days. Dan, however, felt it was time for me to begin using my teaching abilities at Korea Christian College. We each had completed our master's degree while in the States on furlough, and KCC needed me. I resisted teaching college students and argued that I was better suited for elementary school. Soon, however, I was teaching more classes than many of the male missionaries and was deeply involved in training teachers for Korean churches. College teaching gave me a flexible schedule, allowing me to be home when my children were.

Dan and I had decided that missionaries need to be part of the local culture. For that reason, and because it suited us, we lived in a Korean house in a Korean neighborhood; our children went to Korean schools; and we adopted much of the Korean culture. As we opened up to Korea, it opened up to us and led to perhaps the most exciting season of my life. I learned the art of Korean flower arranging and through flower exhibits, made frequent television appearances. I met Korea's First Lady, exchanged gifts with her and had tea with her at the presidential mansion. I even worked for the White House for a day, making flower arrangements for President Lyndon Johnson's reception for the Korean president. I wrote columns for two Korean newspapers, regular articles for an American women's magazine and chapters in three books on Korea. I served as president of the International Women's Association and of the Seoul Garden Club. Invitations to embassy events were frequent. I narrated and participated in fashion shows and once did a commercial for a fertilizer company.

For Korean Christians, my involvement in Korea was seen as a plus, and I will never forget the time I was introduced as "my Korean friend." I did not feel the same support from my fellow missionaries, and even though I continued to teach and work at KCC and to be involved in local church work, I often felt alienated because of the direction my life had taken. One husband even took me aside and asked me not to talk about my activities with his wife because it would make her less content to be just a homemaker.

No One Pattern
Christian women of my generation have bought into a concept of their role that cannot be defined. Many scriptures allude to Christian character but not one defines the characteristics of a Christian woman. There is no one model. Because women tend to compare themselves

with others and to compete rather than cooperate, we do not allow for the individuality and creativity God has given us. Within the context of God's will and direction, each woman must make her own decisions as to who she is and what she will become. This was brought home to me vividly when a missionary friend confessed that she often felt guilty that she was not doing the kinds of outside activities I was involved in, and I admitted to her that I felt I should be more like the homebody she was. God does not expect us to fit into a mold. He expects us to use the opportunities he gives us to the glory of the Kingdom.

On our second furlough, Dan and I went back to school. He earned a doctorate in higher education, and I completed the education specialist degree. Upon our return to Korea, there were school debts to pay, and in order for me to continue to teach at KCC and be involved in the community as I had been, we needed additional funds. The money, about $250 a month, would either have to come from our sponsoring congregation or I would need to get a job. The church opted for me to get a job. It still hurts to think that my contribution was not worth $250!

The disappointment turned to opportunity when I began to teach at the Department of Defense School in Seoul which led to my season as a professional. We returned to the States when our girls were in high school and spent two years in Abilene, where Dan served as missionary-in-residence and I taught at ACU and in the public schools. Even though we loved Abilene, it did not seem to be what God had in mind for us. We prayed that he would place us in the Kingdom where he wanted us (I Cor. 12:18) and investigated every opportunity that presented itself. None worked out until we received a call from Lubbock Christian College. I have to admit that flat, treeless Lubbock was not what I had in mind, but it turned out to be the right place for us, and we spent the next 24 years on the faculty and in the administration at LCU. Dan taught Bible and missions, and I completed my doctorate and taught courses in education. Dan retired as vice president for academic affairs and I ended my tenure as dean of the College of Education.

It was during this professional season of my life that I struggled most with the role of women in the church. When I became one of the first academic deans at a Christian university, some questioned whether it was appropriate. Dan and I were active members of the Broadway Church where he served as an elder and I coordinated the women's ministry. What women could and could not do was certainly an issue to be considered. After studying what the New Testament says on the subject, it has become my belief that women can do anything except be elders, preachers or Bible teachers of Christian males. I do not necessarily understand why those restrictions are placed on women, and I wish the Apostle Paul had been a little clearer on the subject, but I can accept them. From that point on, there is no limit on the use of gifts in God's kingdom.

Even though I cannot be a preacher, I have had wonderful opportunities to develop as a speaker. I began talking at the age of six months and, as my mother often said, I never stopped. As a result of our experiences in Korea, I had written a book titled *Sojourners: Women with a Mission* that was designed to help women overcome the culture shock that is inevitable when living in a foreign country. Because of the book, my first speaking appointments were always titled "Women with a Mission." Then I began to be asked to speak at ladies' days and retreats, and those demanded more than personal experience. With Dan's help, I learned to study the Bible in a deeper and more significant way and looked at invitations to speak as an invitation to learn rather than just to share.

When I became dean of the College of Education at Lubbock Christian University, I had several goals in mind. The first was to have a premier teacher education program, and I believe that was accomplished through a talented and service-oriented faculty. Another was to let others know about LCU, and the best way to do that was to become personally active at the local, state and national level. It meant building partnerships and developing collaboratives at every level. It meant being willing to take the initiative and give the time to serve as a leader at the state level and to be an officer in national organizations. God provided the opportunities and opened the doors.

As a result, I feel my professional season was a winning one, and I had no regrets when I retired.

Missions for Dan and me has not been just a season. Rather it has been more a seasoning that has flavored almost everything we have done. We spent 17 years in Korea and ten summers training future missionaries at the ACU Summer Mission Workshop, and have conducted numerous workshops with churches involved with foreign missions. We have trained mission teams. We have written four books on missions, and I developed a curriculum for teaching missions to children. We have worked on the field with missionaries in South America, Central America, Asia and Europe. We have spent time as missionaries in Kenya and in American Samoa and continue to be involved in South Korea. Our decision to stay at Lubbock Christian University was made because we saw that campus as a mission field.

A Challenging New Season
The seasons have not been without storms. There have been health problems and never enough money. I tend to be emotional and I am a worrier. I have to remind myself that the great commission in Matthew 28:18-20 has directed our lives, and I gain great comfort from the last verse in which Jesus promises to be with us, even to the end of the age.

As I enter a new season of my life, I do not know what the future holds. This new season frightens me more than any of the others. I do not like growing old. I do not like the aches and pains and not being able to do the things I once did so easily. I wonder if we will be able to manage finances with no retirement other than Social Security. I worry about becoming dependent on others and what kind of an old person I will be.

On one hand, there are tremendous blessings. These include three grown daughters who are beautiful both on the inside and outside and whose faith and commitment bring tears to my eyes. They include sons-in-law whom God sent as a direct answer to my prayers that he would prepare husbands for my daughters who would help them grow closer to him. And, of course, there are 11 beautiful grandchildren in whose lives I am privileged to play a part. There is a new house in the hill country of south Texas and the opportunity to make a new life and new friends.

This new season also brings new challenges. There is the opportunity to continue to work part time with teacher educators in a professional capacity and to train teachers of missions in an exciting, organized effort. There has even been a request that we return to Korea on a part-time basis. I am reminded of the old man Caleb in Joshua 14 who demanded that he be given the mountain rather than an easier inheritance, because he felt that he had the strength to conquer it. On the other hand, there was the 80-year-old Barzillai in 2 Samuel 19 who refused to go to Jerusalem with David because he was old and tired, yet was still blessed by David. Whether we are to be Calebs or Barzillais remains to be seen.

I began this account of my spiritual journey by talking about walking to church. That third grader who felt so grown-up being responsible for her sisters had no idea what the future held for her. The 65-year-old she has become does not always feel very grown up, and she knows that she does not know the future. What she does know is that what the elder told her those many years ago is true. God will take care of the rest if we put our trust in him.

Joyce (Smith) Hardin received the B.A. degree from Abilene Christian University and the M.A. degree from Eastern New Mexico University. She earned an Education Specialist degree and a Doctor of Education degree from Oklahoma State University.

Joyce is married to Dan Hardin, and they have three daughers and 11 grandchildren. The Hardins spent 17 years as missionaries to Korea. They joned the faculty of Lubbock Christian University in 1976, where Joyce later served as dean of the College of Education.

She has spoken for many women's programs and lectureships, as well as presented papers at professional conferences. She has authored two books, *Sojourners: Women with a Mission* and *Three Steps Behind.*

5

_____

A Mustard Seed Kind of Faith

Anna M. Griffith

All of us need more faith. We tremble at Jesus' often repeated invective, "O ye of little faith!" Yet, as earnestly as we desire to have strong faith, we all have periods of doubt. At times of great stress in the past few years, I have even cried out, "Today, Lord, I am not sure if I even believe that you exist. Tomorrow, when I have returned to my senses, please forgive me!" This kind of enigmatic prayer reveals two important truths: First, I do believe in God and in my secure relationship with him, even though the here and now fails to reflect that confidence. Second, faith must not and does not rest on feelings. Thus I add my voice to the request of Jesus' disciples in Luke 17:5: "Lord, increase our faith!" (NASB). With great anticipation, I hope, "Wonderful! Now he will tell me how to increase my faith!" But then he delivers what feels like a gentle slap on the hand: "And the Lord said, 'If you had faith like a mustard seed, you would say to this mulberry tree, Be uprooted and be planted in the sea'; and it would obey you" (v. 6).

A mustard seed? How can a mustard seed have faith? If it did, what would a mustard seed "do," if indeed it could "do" anything? Do we not show our faith by our works (James 2:14-18)? At least for the moment, Luke 17:6 was one of those murky passages I was not quite grasping, and maybe never would. But then he tells a parable, perhaps to illuminate the allusion to the mustard seed.

> "But which of you, having a slave plowing or tending sheep, will say to him when he has come in from the field, 'Come immediately and sit down to eat'? But will he not say to him, 'Prepare something for me to eat, and properly clothe yourself and serve me until I have eaten and drunk; and afterward you will eat and drink'?
>
> "He does not thank the slave because he did the things which were commanded, does he? So you too, when you do all the things which are commanded you, say, 'We are unworthy slaves; we have done only that which we ought to have done.'"

A slave? What does this have to do with faith? I hardly wanted to be a servant, much less a slave. Furthermore, if I have done everything I should have done, I wanted to be worthy. I have always wanted to do great things for God. I wanted to be a writer. I wanted to be a great scholar, to teach and write for women's classes, and even perhaps to help break down the church's gender barriers. But this parable haunted me. When I have done all that I could—by my own planning, gut-driven will and determination—would I then really still be an unprofitable servant, Lord? Does this have anything to do with faith?

A Hunger for God's Word
When I was nine years old and feeling a persistent tugging at my heart, I was baptized in Levelland, Texas, by J. V. Davis. In particular, I remember three palpable impressions. First, I felt a pure and indescribable joy. Second, I felt completely and thoroughly cleansed. And third, I had an insatiable desire to read the Bible—a desire which proved to be a constant throughout my life.

I grew up in Levelland, graduated from high school in 1956, attended the Curtis Institute of Music in Philadelphia, and met my husband Carl at church in that city. We married in 1959, moved to Phoenix where Carl took a job with Sperry, had four children (all boys) as fast as we legally could, and took our place in the stream of life. By this time, I had discovered the black holes of the biblical text—Leviticus, Ezekiel, Psalm 119, Hebrews, and Revelation—but I had determined to explore, if not fathom, their depths eventually. I knew they would just take longer.

We lived in Phoenix for 22 years, attending the Camelback Church of Christ most of that time. Our third son, Naasson, was killed in a car/bike accident in 1974. It was the hardest thing we had ever experienced, but the church held us in their arms until we could get warm again. We learned to appreciate the church as never before—God's family being a place where people could heal, Jesus incarnate on earth, God with skin on.

When I realized in 1976 that we would have three children in college at once, I re-enrolled in college myself to acquire a degree in mathematics, thinking I would go to work to help with finances. Grand Canyon College, a Baptist school, was the closest to us, so I enrolled there. I took the Bible survey courses required of all freshmen, but concentrated on mathematics. However, God worked on me through this school. It offered a course in "Biblical Backgrounds" taught by J. Niles Puckett. Dr. Puckett had traveled extensively in the Holy Land, had taken many pictures, loved biblical archaeology (as I did), and was much loved by his students. After one semester, I joined their ranks.

Dr. Puckett was also the Greek professor. After three years of passing the Greek rooms where students were laboring over their alphas and omegas, the text began tugging at me from a different direction. GCC had the only Greek chair in Arizona. Why not take Greek while it was so handy?

I took Greek for two years, continuing for a year after I had graduated in mathematics. By that time, biblical studies held me completely and permanently captive. In 1983, Carl transferred from Sperry in Phoenix to Sperry in Albuquerque. Since I had been teaching ladies' Bible classes, and some of the material I had written was being published,[1] I decided that if I were to continue to teach adults and write materials, I should acquire all the tools possible. Thus I began taking the textual studies offered by Bill Robinson at the Christian Student

Center at the University of New Mexico. After a year, Bill sent me to Abilene Christian University to study under "your people," as he put it.

With short courses, independent studies and two semesters on campus, I earned a master's degree in Biblical and Related Studies in May, 1987. In the fall of that year, I went with 15 other students to Jerusalem to study for a semester, returning from Jerusalem wanting nothing more than to continue studying. Unfortunately, New Mexico had no resources for other graduate-level Bible courses, and I did not want to leave my long-suffering husband again.

I finally prayed, "Lord, if this longing is from me, it will pass. If it is from you, you will just have to work it out, because I am not leaving my husband again." Telling God what he should do probably is never appropriate, but I am convinced that he honors our weaknesses and limitations if we confess them in sincerity. I know he honors marriage. In the meantime, ACU had opened an extension in Albuquerque, so I availed myself of some of those textual courses.

Carl and I loved living in Albuquerque. Differing cultures give the city an incomparable ambiance. We could hike in lush alpine forests at 10,000 feet altitude within 45 minutes. The city is large enough to offer urban amenities, but intimate enough to traverse with ease. The four seasons were a refreshing change from Phoenix.

Our youngest son, Clark, had moved to Albuquerque from Philadelphia where he had been attending Curtis Institute of Music, and it was a joy to have him living in the same city. Sean, his "significant other," joined him soon after he arrived. Although Carl and I have never approved of the homosexual lifestyle, we nonetheless deeply loved and enjoyed both of these talented young men.

God's Ways

Halfway through 1988, Bell Helicopter began wooing Carl to come to work in Fort Worth. We did not want to move. I was on a first-name basis with rocks and trees on Trail 103 on Sandia Crest. The last time I walked that trail, I cried. And then I remembered my prayer. Dallas/Fort Worth—home to at least four major theological seminaries, libraries and conferences—and just three hours from Abilene. What was I thinking? I wasn't! We moved in May, 1989, setting up our nest in Colleyville. The same month that we moved, ACU closed the extension courses in Albuquerque and opened a series in Dallas. Truly, God moves in mysterious ways.

Because my mother, born in 1903, was no longer able to live alone, my brother John and his wife Fran moved from their home in Lubbock to Levelland to care for her. I began visiting West Texas on a regular basis to help out. On one of these trips, I stopped at ACU to check something on my transcript. The advisor for the Master of Divinity students, and the director of the Doctor of Ministry program, told me within ten minutes of each other that I should pursue the Master of Divinity because I was so close to completing the requirements anyway. My first impression was that it was one of the silliest things I ever heard. "Now what would I do with that?!" I asked one of them.

He snapped back, "Why don't you let God decide that?!" I assured them I would think about it, but thought to myself, "This is ridiculous!" That same month we received a chatty letter from Clark that closed, "Well, at least now it's official. Sean has AIDS, and I am HIV-positive." My world was in chaos. Not since Naasson's death had I felt completely shattered. I begged Clark to run, not walk, to God—not on his own terms, not on my terms, not on those of the church in which he grew up, but on God's terms. He quietly responded, "Mom, the church isn't doing anything about AIDS." I said nothing; he was right. But then I knew. Within two months, I began work on the Master of Divinity. None of the study had been a lark.

In the 1980s our society was growing aware of the AIDS phenomenon. Along with other conservatives, I had been repulsed with the "in your face" victim mentality of the militant activists and privately grateful that I did not need to deal with these issues. I wanted to write for and teach in the cloistered community of the church. AIDS was not my problem. However, as more and more stories circulated about churches closing their doors on their own who were affected by AIDS, the problem came closer. I began to think, "There but for the grace of God, go I." When Clark disclosed his seropositivity, reality closed in: "There go I."

I knew nothing about AIDS. However, one of my M. Div. ministry courses in 1993 was "Seminar on Death and Dying," taught by Dr. Bruce Davis. For my paper, he graciously granted permission to write on AIDS—a first for his classes. The paper was difficult to write, but very well received. During this winter semester, Sean died. As grief for him, as well as a growing grief for my still healthy son, began to envelop me, Dr. Davis's class became my support group.

Beginning a Ministry

In confidence, I had told our pulpit minister, Rick Atchley, and Lynn Lovell, one of our elders, that our son was HIV-positive. Both were very supportive. Lynn requested a copy of my paper, which he duplicated for the other elders. Within six months, both asked if we would begin an AIDS ministry, to which we assented. We held some classes on Wednesday nights, conducted some seminars, handed out literature, and helped a few families who had already lost family members, but no people living with AIDS came to us. One of our stated goals was to build a bridge between the Richland Hills Church and the AIDS community, but my growing impression was that we were building the bridge beginning in the center of the span.

In the meantime, my academic focus turned increasingly toward AIDS. Finishing the M.Div. in 1995, I was accepted into the doctoral program at ACU, partly because of the AIDS ministry. All of us—the ACU faculty, the leadership at Richland Hills, and my family—wanted the AIDS ministry structured on as solid a foundation as possible. I participated in a support group through Fort Worth's AIDS Outreach Center (AOC) and worked on a care team with AIDS Interfaith Network (AIN), partly to work through my own grief, but partly to learn.

While we were teaching the Wednesday night AIDS lessons, one of the members at Richland Hills brought his nephew "Steven" to us. Steve was a resident of Samaritan House, an AIDS shelter in northwest Fort Worth. He had AIDS, but he had come back to the Lord and wanted to work with us in this ministry. However, Steve was sicker than we thought. I visited him a few times at Samaritan House, but he died within weeks.

After Steve died, I had no concrete link with Samaritan House. Our ministry team tried to hold mini-worship services there, but we were voted out. The residents did not want "Bible beaters" pushing religion down their throats. None of us wanted to do that anyway. But how could we reach Samaritan House?

The first principle of ministry is to meet people where they are, not where you wish them to be. The Samaritan House residents seemed to be daring us to meet them where they were—certainly an alien world for most of us. Jesus enjoined us to give "a cup of cold water," but cold water they had. I searched my soul. If I had AIDS, was convinced that not a drop of genuine love was left in this world, was rejected by family, friends and churches, what could build a bridge between me and a person who genuinely cared?

In May 1996, I rolled up my sleeves, marched into my kitchen, baked a big batch of made-from-scratch chocolate chip cookies, and drove to Samaritan House. On the way, I prayed fervently, "Lord, help me to see everyone I meet the way you see them. Let them see you in me—not me, but you. And Lord, no matter what happens, may you be glorified above all."

If I offer you a cookie, it could mean we have something in common. If it is straight from the oven and made from scratch, it says I care. If I give it to you straightforwardly, with a smile but few words, it conveys that I have no hidden agenda. If I do it the same way, same day of the week, same time of day, week after week, it conveys the message that I seek a relationship. And a grandmotherly demeanor can't hurt.

I walked in, cookies in hand, offered one to every person I saw, left the rest of the cookies and went home. The first few times I did it, people had the funniest expressions. All expressed surprise that the cookies were homemade. After six weeks, someone asked, "Why are you doing this?" I could only answer, "Because God loves you." After three months, someone finally asked my name. Of course, by that time, it was a moot question, because everyone just called me "Cookie Lady." If someone has AIDS, building trust with them is a tedious, time-consuming, patience-challenging process.

I finished my Doctor of Ministry from ACU in 1998.[2] The Richland Hills church ran a continuous ad in the *Christian Chronicle* asking, "How can we help you in the AIDS crisis?" which drew requests from all over the United States and many foreign countries, but ministry within the congregation was still limited. I was learning that, in a religious context at least, AIDS is a long-distance ministry. People feel safer calling or writing from out of state than they do closer to home. Larry Holmes (Abilene), Larry James (Dallas), and Larry Calvin (Richland Hills Church) all encouraged me with what I now call "The Larry Principle": People from the church will not come to you until they see you ministering to people from the outstide.

Seeking Faith

Daily I asked the Lord to show me the way. Daily I wondered what I should be doing differently. I wrote the ministry model in a form that we could give our missionaries so they would be equipped to meet AIDS on the mission field, and I continued to take cookies every week. Some of the times I took cookies, I was shunned. Occasionally, I simply did not even see another person—staff or resident. I still waited for a ministry to reach AIDS patients through the church. I was spending myself in doing what I thought I should, but seemed to be getting nowhere. Feeling completely unprofitable, I finally prayed, "Lord increase my faith!"

Only in the synoptic gospels do we find Jesus' mustard seed parables. With only minor variations, his parable comparing the size of the kingdom of heaven to a mustard plant occurs in Matthew 13:31f, Mark 4:30ff, and Luke 13:18f. The nature and role of faith are not what Jesus emphasizes in these passages, but in Matthew 17:19-20, issues of faith are crucial. Jesus rebuked that generation (or the faith-deficient disciples?) for their unbelief.[3] I did not understand how a mustard seed could have "faith." It could not. I went to the store and bought some mustard seeds, brought them home, opened the package and spread a few out on a paper towel. I looked at them. Finally, I bit into one. It tasted like mustard.

I tried to imagine myself as a mustard seed. What would I do?

What are mustard seeds good for? I finally decided that, if I were a mustard seed, I would have at least one—and perhaps three—functions, none of which would be mine to decide. First, I could be left in a jar on a shelf somewhere to be used at the discretion of my owner. Or, I might be ground up, eventually to grace someone's hot dog at a Fourth of July backyard barbecue. Finally, I might be planted in the ground, cultivated and watered, so I might grow into a mustard tree, eventually reproducing myself—all at the discretion of my owner. I would have no say. If I were actually to be used, I would lose my identity as a seed and emerge either as mustard or a mustard plant.

But what of the nature of my faith as a mustard seed? That is more problematic. The only thing resembling faith that I would possess as a mustard seed is my genetic code, which would determine both my character (I would taste like mustard when crushed) and my seed-like ability to reproduce. Therefore, if I acted on this kind of faith, I would be faithful to perform the master's bidding, either to yield my flavor or to shed my seed identity and grow to become a plant—all at the discretion of my owner.

At this point in the fanciful meanderings, I, like the recalcitrant disciples, was still struggling with my "little" faith. Like a typical Christian, I wanted to have strong faith—bigger, greater faith—so I could move mountains for God. But how could a mustard seed have great quantities of faith? Its "faith" could only be simple, focused on seasoning and reproduction. Like countless others, I had read the mustard seed parables with a view toward the size of faith. However, the translations varied with enough regularity that I was drawn inexorably back to the original language. The Greek in both Matthew 17:20 and Luke 17:6 would render the translation, "If you have faith as (or, like) a grain of mustand seed...."[4] There is no indication of "faith the size of a mustard seed" (*NRSV*) or "faith as small as a mustard seed" (*NIV*). Surely it is the character of faith that Jesus is stressing to his apostles, not the size of their faith. Like his apostles, I was asking Jesus to increase the size of my faith, but he was actually storing me in a jar on the shelf until he chose to use me.

The Faithfulness of the Father

The "faith" of a mustard seed is negligible compared with that of a faith-ful disciple. Yet the size of faith—even if it be tiny—can never be com-pared to the one in whom the disciple has faith. His faithfulness is the key to success. Even if I have faith the size of a mustard seed, it returns me to the throne of the one possessing infinite faithfulness. If I have faith the character of a mustard seed, it simply subsumes my identity to that of the master, moving me unquestioningly to do his bidding.

Many scholars believe that the metaphor of the mustard seed and the parable of the unprofitable servant are two disconnected sayings of Jesus, but I am convinced that the latter illustrates in human terms the more abstract principle of the former. Regardless, I concur with most assessments that it is a difficult, if not obscure, parable.

I was beginning to identify strongly with this pitiable slave. The man simply cannot be successful. He strives, works, groans under the load, and comes in at the end of the day—hot, sweaty and exhausted. Then he must clean up, prepare the master's dinner, serve him, eat something if anything is left over, and go to bed. Even after all of that, he has only done the requirements of one day's work. As he falls exhausted on the bed, his last thought is that he must follow the same unprofitable regi-men—from his perspective—the next day and the next.

But what is the picture from the master's perspective? Likely he has other slaves with other tasks. He sees the bigger picture. He orchestrates these tasks to accomplish a greater whole—an end result. The harvest will come. There will be a festival. All can rejoice togeth-er that they have reached a common goal.

In order to do all that he does with so little reward, the servant must have faith of the character of the mustard seed. His is the unquestion-ing and simple faith in the master that his work will be made worthy because of his dependence on the trustworthiness of the master.

I was learning these lessons because I had no choice. I had prayed, "Lord, increase my faith"; so instead of making my faith larg-er, God began changing its character. For two years, I was stored in a spiritual jar in the cellar, waiting for the master's timing. However, I was also being crushed to grace the spiritual barbecues of the AIDS

70

community. Eventually, the seed was also planted. That seed has ceased to be a seed, but neither is it yet a fully grown tree.

If I give a cup of cold water—or a cookie—in his name, he assures me that it will be rewarded. Mother Teresa reminded us that God never commands us to be successful, only faithful. In these kinds of ministries, gender issues and status in the church are irrelevant. If a person—male or female, old or young, married or single—will prepare himself or herself to be God's person, he will create a way to use that preparedness. If the person ascribes importance to any of these other issues, he or she does not possess mustard-seed faith, but has taken his or her eyes off the master.

Principles of Ministry

The first principle of ministry is to meet people where they are. The second is that all ministry is God's ministry, not ours. The importance of ministry depends not on position in the church, on recognition, on numbers or salary, but on fidelity to the master. These other things are human measures of worth, not divine assessments. The parable of the unprofitable servant teaches several important lessons. Most obvious is that of unquestioning faithfulness to the master, to value above all else the fact of his lordship. Also, the master owes his servants nothing—not comfort, wealth or success. The parable rules out any view of a merited reward, but must depend on whatever reward the master may give. Reward cannot be earned. It depends on the will of the master.

Taken together, the two parables teach a liberating lesson. The largest promise applies even to the smallest faith. The size of faith gives way to the question of whether there is true faith at all—a faith which, forgetting itself, focuses completely on its object, and in keeping with James 2:14-18, the unprofitable servant shows his faith by his works.

Having a mustard-seed kind of faith, may we all clothe ourselves with the mantle of the "unprofitable servant" in order that his blazing glory may be seen throughout the world.

As this essay is being prepared (Fall 2000), Clark Griffith is thriving in the California Bay Area, preparing a public recital from the works of Bach, Shubert and Barber. The master has blessed the AIDS ministry by giving us this son for many more years than we could have expected, and for that, we can only fall to our knees with gratitude.

Notes

1 *Balance: A Modern Christian Challenge* (1981) and *From Paul to Philippi with Love* (1984).

2. The title of my project thesis was "Implementing an AIDS Ministry Model Inside and Outside the Congregation."

3. The parallel passage in Mark 9:14-29 which omits the mustard seed saying also demonstrates the necessity of faith.

4. So *KJV, RSV,* and *NASV.*

Anna Griffith has been married to Carl Griffith, an avionics engineer with Bell Helicopter, for 42 years. They have three sons and four grand-children, and are active members of the Richland Hills Church of Christ in Fort Worth, Texas.

Anna's hobbies include the needle arts and "town planning," as a collec-tor of Dept. 56's "Dickens Village." In 1995 she completed the Master of Divinity degree, and in 1998 the Doctor of Ministry degree from Abilene Christian University.

6

The Abundant Life

Josephine Decierdo-Mock

I was raised in the migrant camps and housing projects of Oxnard, California—one of four children of a Filipino-born father and a Mexican-born mother. My father came over by ship in the 1920s, lured by America's riches, only to spend the next 40 years as a migrant worker. He had been a primary school teacher in his native Philippines, trained to be one when he was only in the eighth grade because of his knowledge of the English language. My mother had a second-grade education and knew only Spanish when she entered the U.S. illegally at the age of 18. My father was 28 years older than she was. Working alongside Mexicans, my father learned some Spanish, and along the way my mother learned some English and my father's language.

I have often been asked which culture I gravitated toward. Did I feel Mexican, Mexican-American, Filipino or American? What language did I speak at home, my mother's or my father's? Does culture matter in the life of a Christian? Without my father, we spent hot summers and cold winters in Mexico with my mother's family. Other times, we visited and ate with the Filipinos in the Oxnard Filipino camps. I grew up with soul and Latin music, ate homemade tortillas and rice and U.S. commodities.

My mother was a Catholic, and my father professed to be one but never did any of the rituals. Their lack of acceptance of each other's differences, their lack of understanding in numerous ways, and their lack of basic communication tools led to terrible domestic abuse (physical, emotional and mental) on an almost daily basis. But we never went hungry or unclothed

There were no appropriate role models at home for me, my two sisters and my brother. I withdrew into my own world, using the Catholic religion, sports, school and friends as means of escape, masking depression with apparent optimism and smiles. During my teen years, I even contemplated suicide, but I was afraid I'd go to hell. Afraid and depressed, I prayed for a way out.

Filling My Heart, Setting Me Free

On my way to Mass and confession several times a week, I would pass a small storefront church, a black congregation. I became friends with the minister, who eventually asked me to translate some Christian tracts from English to Spanish. I did that during my senior year of high school, and the summer after graduation I became a Christian. God knew I was searching, and he showed me the way in his perfect time. I continued praying, thanking the Lord for filling the emptiness of my heart and lifting my burden.

God gave me new life, lifting me to a higher plane. I was transformed from a withdrawn, timid 18-year-old with poor self esteem into the daughter of a King! When I acknowledge God's presence, have faith and obey him, he gives me the abundant life he speaks of in John 10:10. It is humbling that God in his infinite goodness chose me. I truly believe he was with me and continues to be with me, and I am forever indebted to him.

I was not aware that my upbringing, race, social status, poverty and sex were factors the world considered when viewing me. I became aware of them as the years went by, but they are a part of my life, and I use them for God's glory, becoming "all things to all men so that by all possible means I might save some." My affirmation comes from God, not from men or women, and my self-worth comes from knowing I am his. Christ has set me free!

Today, the politically correct way of saying where I came from is that I am a "survivor." I do not like the term, because it reeks of pity, and I don't want sympathy. As we look at Jesus' life, he would have been a fitting object for pity. He never asked for it; it would have been an insult. Instead, he served.

For me, it is not a matter of survival; it is a matter of being a disciple of Jesus and making choices and decisions based on my relationship with him. He permits me to go through trials to show that he is in control, that he knows what is best for me, and that I should trust him. Just as I overcame my past, I know that hope is available to all, especially women who feel trapped, hopeless and worthless.

Too often women walk though life using the past, their problems, their socio-economic status and their culture as a crutch. Minority women "play the race card" and make excuses for their behavior. We limit God's power in our lives because of the bitterness, hate and pride in our hearts. To say there is no solution or possibility of change is blasphemous and limits the power of the Spirit within us.

Growing Together

When I was 18, I suffered the consequences of a bad decision. My daughter Evette was born. What should I tell people when I share my Christianity with them, then mention that I am unmarried with a child? I struggled with the thought that I would be seen as a hypocrite. God had forgiven my sin, and it was time to move on with my life. I used my situation as an opportunity to show that I had learned from my mistake. I suffered. I had to work, and I did not want to end up in the fields or on welfare.

With my parents' help in taking care of my child, and with determination and God, I was able to graduate from Pepperdine with a teaching credential. Have we forgotten that God is more forgiving than we are toward ourselves and others?

I have indeed been blessed. My daughter has been an example for me and my family, because she exhibits a heart of love and service and a radiance that only a committed child of God can have.

A Christian counselor once told me that I had to choose whether to have the type of marriage my parents had or one that was different.

75

I need to let the past go, yet sometimes I find myself living it again. Instead of having an attitude of "I'll show you!" it should be, "Show me, Lord, please!" My attitude has to be different if I profess to be a Christian and want to have an impact on the women around me, both Christian and non-Christian.

God blessed me with a husband who is a devoted Christian. We have different personalities, but we believe God made us for each other. It has not been easy because of our differences, but Steve has helped me in my spiritual walk, and I have helped him. Since we did not grow up in Christian homes, we have had to learn to be Christian parents and role models for our three children. Instead of manipulation, screaming, control and hate, I should communicate, share and love, and I can only learn to do that if I am a disciple of Jesus. I have to decide to live a different life from the one I grew up with, just as I have to decide to follow Christ and his teachings. Our family is built on Christian principles. We are close-knit; we enjoy being together; and we are forming traditions we will pass on.

I have been asked: "What made you, your husband and your family become missionaries?" My response is that we did not become missionaries. It was an extension and continuation of our lives in the U.S. Both of us, before we met each other and after we married, traveled in different parts of the world. Steve, in his search for truth, was converted in Israel, returned to the U.S., and graduated from a preaching school. I was impressed with the tanned surfer who was a bit of a rebel and liked to rock the boat. As a woman, I complement Steve. I am not the risk-taker he is.

After we married, we worked among the Latinos in Encinitas, Escondido and other parts of north San Diego County. We did this in addition to teaching in public schools. For years, we prayed for God to show us if he wanted us to stay in our "comfort zone" in America or to go abroad. Would we give up our good teaching jobs, a house with a pool, my women's soccer team, our children's activities and friends, Steve's surfing? I had to be a disciple, a follower, a learner in my own backyard first. Regardless of who or where I am, I have a mission.

Steve and I took into consideration the impact our decision would have on our daughter and two sons. What good is it if I bring others to Christ and neglect my own children? It takes time, energy, wisdom, love and patience to teach them by words and example. All three are faithful Christians, using their unique personalities and talents to touch their friends' lives.

To be a woman in ministry, I must first be a disciple. Discipleship and ministry go hand in hand. They are my life, and they are full time. I hear men share deep insights about God and his Word, encouraging me to put them into action. Why do women wait? We have tremendous and numerous talents, so let us be initiators!

The Need for Discipleship
The word disciple appears 269 times in the New Testament. Jesus said in Matthew 28:19, "Go therefore and make disciples of all nations, baptizing them in the name of the Father and of the Son and of the Holy Spirit, teaching them to obey everything I have commanded you." Churches involved in missions tend to gauge success by the number baptized, but many new Christians fall away if they have been discipled to the church rather than to Jesus. Jesus worked with 12 men, and of those, he was especially close to three.

In my 30 years as a Christian, I have visited many churches in the U.S., Europe, South America, Mexico and the Philippines. Each is unique. But at some point over the centuries, we failed to make discipleship a condition of being a Christian. We haven't required following Jesus in his example, spirit and teachings. Today's churches are filled with undiscipled Christians. We focus on tradition, opinion and self rather than on being servants and reaching the lost, the mission Jesus gave us. Is Jesus Lord? He cannot be my Lord if I am not a disciple.

Was it easier to be a disciple during Jesus' time? A woman could accompany him with an attitude of study, obedience and imitation. She knew what to do and what it would cost. She had to be with him to learn to do what he did. Of course, it cannot be the same today, but the priorities and intentions of my heart as a disciple can and should remain the same.

In my heart, there is a desire to be like Jesus. It is my intent to become more like him, so I live my life accordingly. It is a decision I made years ago. If I am a disciple, learning from Jesus, it becomes obvious to my friends, my neighbors, my colleagues at work, and especially my family. I can study the Word, obey Jesus and imitate him today.

Romans 12:2 says: "Do not conform any longer to the pattern of this world, but be transformed by the renewing of your mind. Then you will be able to test and approve what God's will is (what God wants from me here and now)—his good (which leads to my spiritual and moral growth), pleasing (to God, not necessarily to me), and perfect (no improvement can be made on it) will."

I depend totally on God. I am assured that, when I make a decision based on my relationship with him, he is faithful and will work it out in a way that is best for me, even if my decision is a bad one and not according to his will.

Asking Questions

God has a wonderful way of putting our talents or gifts to work. Perhaps they are hidden from us. He brings us into situations and watches our reactions and responses. At times, I am sure he is disappointed. Other times, he must be amused. His love and patience have changed me from a pessimist to an optimist. My countenance has changed, and I enjoy being with people. Where once I hid my life from them and interacted on a superficial level, God has taught me to be open. Once, I resisted openness because it would make me vulnerable, but God wants me to ask deep questions of people. He wants me to listen and get involved in their lives, genuinely caring like God, "who comforts us in all our troubles, so we can comfort those in any trouble with the comfort we ourselves have received from God" (2 Cor. 1:4).

I am a witness for Christ and his sacrifice. He is carrying out his purpose through me as a woman. My heart and demeanor should be visible to those around me. At times, I have been guilty of compartmentalizing my life as a Christian—being one way with my husband, another way with family or friends, different at work, at church, in crowds. I don't think Christ had that in mind for us. I am to walk in step with the Spirit and become an open letter to everyone around me, no matter where I am or whom I am with.

It hasn't always been that way. When I first became a Christian, I felt a sense of duty to convert people to gain favor with God. It was a carryover from my previous religion. If I confess my sins to the priest and go to mass enough times, I am guaranteed entrance into heaven because I am good.

When I look at the life of Jesus, I see that he started conversations with people on common ground and always asked questions. He required the person to think and choose either to reject or accept him. But Jesus never pushed anyone to make a decision. I try to do the same thing. Once some people jokingly asked me how I knew so much about a person. I ask, I listen, I try to fill in the holes.

Working for the church requires great faith and reliance on God. Financial support is not guaranteed with so many issues and traditions distracting and dividing the church. In 1996, we returned from the foreign mission field, wounded in spirit due to some unfortunate situations, but we came away with unforgettable memories of loving Christians and great adventures.

During our transition time in Lubbock, Texas (ten months of considering whether to return to South America or some other part of the world—even whether to go back to the mission field or return to teaching in the public schools in California), my husband worked as a substitute teacher, and I became a volunteer in the community outreach program—Inside Out—supported by the Central Church. People would come in daily asking for food and clothing, medical and spiritual help. I believed the people when they said that you can be homeless from one day to the next. We were not in a good financial situation ourselves, and I knew it was true.

I would go with another worker to the county jail to visit women and study with them. Most were there on drug-related charges. I was scared at first, because I didn't know how the ladies would treat me. My co-worker said it would be fine. "Just be yourself, because these ladies can tell if you're genuine and really concerned about them."

They opened their hearts, and I learned to listen. They wanted someone who would listen and not judge. They yearned for freedom from jail and their addictions, but they knew they had to be spiritually free first. Every time I went into the jail, I was a little scared as I heard the numerous doors shut loudly behind me. Sometimes the dynamics among the ladies in the musty room where we held our sessions were not positive, and I'd fear getting caught in the middle with no way out. But God took care of me! Those were some of the most rewarding months of my life. I came away humbled and more compassionate.

God's Surprising Guidance
Coming off the mission field and rethinking what road to take was difficult, but God continually teaches us. He works through people, and this time he used my daughter. She reminded us that secular jobs are always available, but an opportunity to work in God's kingdom with a wonderful Christian team did not come often. If we were trying to follow God's direction for our lives, praying and waiting for his timing, he would bless us. And he did!

In 1997, we were reminded of a team in Tijuana, Baja California, Mexico, consisting of some longtime friends from Escondido. They had left as missionaries to Tijuana the year before we left for South America. Tijuana? I have learned not to say, "I will never do this, never go there," because God makes his plans known to us to show us who is in control. When I put my faith in man, I will be disappointed. Not so with God.

We are very happy that he put us in Mexico. For three years we worked with a godly Christian team. Those three families have returned to the U.S., having served as vocational missionaries for six to eight years. Wherever they go, those families will be blessed, because they love Jesus and believe in seeking, saving and discipling the lost. We love and appreciate our Mexican brothers and sisters for opening their hearts to us and making us feel welcome.

Presently, I am working as a public school teacher in a year-round elementary school just across the border in California. While I was working in the classroom during lunchtime, my teaching partner would come often to visit. We would talk and listen to each other. One day she said, "Don't take offense, but you don't fit the typical picture of a minister's wife. You're a school teacher, you play soccer, you have cool children, and you're not always serious!" I was amused, but glad she felt comfortable enough to say it. She and her husband have since become Christians.

I know whom I belong to! Being a preacher's wife and having a role to fill does not limit my potential as a woman. I have heard Christian wives say, "I belong to so and so," as if they had no identity apart from their husbands! Sometimes that comes from being insecure in your person. But we as women are very special. Jesus saw the goodness and the potential in the heart of each woman he met. So don't put me in a box or label or categorize me.

Losing Focus

One way we can lose focus on Christ is to emphasize the traditions of a particular nation or culture. I am a disciple of Jesus wherever I go. The parameters of my ministry have no limits. The key to the missionary message is Jesus Christ crucified. My message is not patriotic, not respective of nations and individuals, men or women. I am not here to proclaim my own point of view. I am here to proclaim him and not forget that his sacrifice on the cross set me free from sin and the traditions of my former religion. Because of God's love and grace, I am where I am. I rejoice!

Our life is with the Christians in Tijuana. I rotate in the women's class and am currently teaching children and teens on Sunday mornings. I have studied with numerous women about becoming Christians. Those who have decided recently to follow Jesus are serious about their relationship with him, and they share their faith with others. I am not in the business of exporting American church traditions and interpretations south of the border or 6,000-10,000 miles across the Pacific Ocean, though it has happened over and over again.

For example, at the funeral of one of our older faithful members, we were led in singing by members of other congregations. The songs came from the blue songbook translated into Spanish from English.

The pace was so slow and sad that half of us were crying because of the tempo and the antiquity of the words. Those same songs are often used in worship services that feel like a funeral instead of a celebration. I am glad that, in our congregation, we have started to sing contemporary, upbeat songs, sometimes with a small praise group. I am comfortable enough to teach a song where we raise our hands to praise God. It has nothing to do with doctrine or salvation, though in the past it was presented that way. As one brother said, "You Americans are the ones who taught us!"

I also recall an incident in the Philippines last year. After the Lord's Supper, a visiting American preacher scolded the Filipinos for singing during communion, stating that brethren in the U.S. would be offended and that we should study the Bible in depth over this issue. I hid my indignation at the remark. The sisters looked my way, because I had just given a class emphasizing devotion to Jesus, not traditions. I doubt he knew I was American, but I felt bad for the Filipinos who were gracious enough to let some "unknown" impart the Word to them. It was not a problem or an issue for them. The good thing about these people and those we worship with in Tijuana is that they know the emphasis is on proclaiming Jesus. One of our goals in working with this church is to teach them to read and search God's Word for depth and truth.

Looking to God

Another way we can lose focus is to allow the needs of the people to overshadow the message of Christ until sympathy overwhelms us. People's needs are enormous, their situations are complicated, and it is possible to forget why we are there. When the three missionary families left at various times, the young Metro church felt the impact each time. The members felt they were being abandoned. But those in leadership positions reminded them that the missionaries were not their saviors and encouraged them to look to God and put their faith in him. We constantly remind them with gentle words that neither I nor my husband nor any other human being can fulfill their spiritual needs. We are committed to bringing our brothers and sisters to maturity in this respect, and I am happy to say that these people are humble, willing and eager to grow in their relationship with God.

My journey continues, and I feel that life without God is meaningless and without purpose. God has been watching out for me since birth, and he singled me out, let me go through trials and joys, to carry out his work. God engineers my circumstances so I will know him. Of course, he has given me free will, and I must confess that it is difficult at times to obey him. Sometimes my emotions take control, and I rebel and sin. I am not perfect, which is why I need the Lord Jesus.

I am a disciple, continually striving to be able to say with a writer from centuries past, I have abiding peace, the peace of God which transcends all understanding (Phil. 4:7). I have a life now permeated by love. I have a faith that sees everything in light of God's goodness. I have a hope that stands firm in the most discouraging of circumstances. I have the power to do what is right and withstand the forces of evil. I have the abundant life Jesus came to bring.

He sets me free, and his Spirit gives me the power to live in him, learning meekness and lowliness of heart that brings rest to my soul.

Josephine Decierdo-Mock became a Christian in 1970. She spent two years at the University of California at Santa Barbara and received her B.A. and teaching credential from Pepperdine.

She and her husband Steve have three children, Evette, Steven and Joseph.

Josie plays soccer year round. She has traveled to ten Eastern and Western European countries as well as the Philippines, Ecuador, Peru and Chile. Where ever she goes, she meets with and encourages Christians.

7

A Grandmother's Legacy

Holly Catterton Allen

Grandmother Imboden[1] was my first and greatest teacher. I stayed with her for two summers when I was 5 and 6, while my mother (her daughter) finished her college degree.

During those summers our days followed a similar pattern. Every morning we would rise early and prepare an enormous lunch for Grandpa to take out to the cotton fields. Then we would cook eggs, bacon, biscuits, and gravy for breakfast. Grandpa would leave for the day and Grandma and I would begin the daily chores, washing dishes, sweeping the floor, gathering the eggs, feeding the chickens. Afterwards Grandma washed clothes and hung them outside, and then we ironed yesterday's wash. Grandma let me iron the (pre-permapress) pillowcases and Grandpa's enormous handkerchiefs.

Around 10:00 Grandma and I would go into the living room where she would sit in her small gold chair, put her feet on the low padded ottoman, and reach beside the chair for the massive, gold-edged Bible that always sat there. I would pull up a three-legged stool and sit at her feet and watch the minute hand go around the clock while she studied. It lasted one hour. I would stare at the oval-framed picture of Grandpa's stern-faced mother, study the glass knic-knacs in the bric-a-brac shelves on the wall, and follow the antics of the tiny blue butterflies on the clover outside the window.

At precisely 11:00, Grandmother would close her Bible and ask if I was ready to play Parcheesi. We would play for an hour, eat lunch, and then begin the afternoon's chores—bringing in the clothes, watering the hydrangea bushes and peonies, weeding the vegetable garden, etc.

I remember those days with delight. But the hour-long Bible study stands out particularly in my memory. Grandma taught the Ladies' Bible Class at the Hickory Ridge Church of Christ for decades. She is still lovingly remembered by that congregation. The time she spent daily in the Word empowered and enabled those years of teaching and left a legacy among those beloved brothers and sisters.

Years of Orientation

It was two decades later that I attended my first Ladies' Bible Class. I spent those 20 years learning who I was, what I believed, and why. I grew up in Arkansas near Harding College. I had good Christian parents who instructed me in the ways of God. We always went to church. We attended every night of the annual gospel meetings, often conducted by Jerry Jones. We drove to Memphis, Tennessee for the great evangelistic gatherings in the Coliseum, conducted for several years by Jimmy Allen.

I was baptized when I was 10 and I never doubted that I understood salvation. I read my Bible every night and memorized scores of scriptures. I learned the arguments for why we were right on everything (and why everyone else was wrong). By the time I graduated from high school I was sure of who God was, I knew what Christianity was, and I knew exactly what I needed to do to get to heaven: I had to read my Bible, pray, be a good wife, teach a Bible class, teach people about Jesus. All of this I could do (so I thought); I felt very secure (and very smug).

In 1969 I began my freshman year at Harding College, taking Bible courses from Neale Pryor, Alan Isom, Jimmy Allen, Jerry Jones, and the great Andy T. Ritchie. I memorized more scripture and learned more arguments. I also gained a deeper appreciation for the breadth and depth of scripture, its beauty and diversity.

After graduating from Harding, marrying, teaching school for a few years, and having our first child, I had the opportunity to do what

I had wanted to do for years—join the women of the church who met each week for Bible study and fellowship. It was a joy to me to hear women speak of their many years of love for God and their service in his kingdom. I joined them in planning baby and bridal showers, caring for the widows, and taking food to the bereaved and ill. But the best part was the Bible study itself.

Though I was part of the group only one year before we moved away, one moment stands out. The topic was heaven, and several women had spoken when Dorothy Simpson rose and told us of her desire to join God in heaven; she quoted the song "One Sweetly Solemn Thought" which meant so much to her—"Today I'm nearer to my home, than e'er I've been before." She spoke with such a light in her eye, such fervor, I could tell that she truly longed to be there, not necessarily later—sooner would be okay.

That moment has lingered with me, not only the intensity of her desire, but also my reaction: I wasn't ready to go be with God. I was very content right here. A few weeks after that day I spoke with Dorothy about her desire to be with God—and my lack of desire. She comforted me by saying that she felt that her major work on earth was done, that she was willing to stay and do whatever other work God had for her, but she was ready to join him any time. Then she looked at me and said, "You are just beginning the work God has given you. No wonder you are not anxious to leave that work. Be content to do the work he gives you now; when your work is done, you will be ready to go."

I had known in my mind that the earth is not my home—that heaven is my home, but I had not discussed the implications of this theological truth with anyone before. Dorothy's insight and understanding touched me.

Years of Disorientation

Other women I knew in my 20s also began to open new spiritual worlds for me. Jo Childress in Memphis spoke about God in a different way from what I was used to. She would say, "I believe the Lord is telling me to do this or that." I had never heard anyone talk this way;

I was uncomfortable around her but intrigued. Then I came to know Pat Griffith. She taught the Sunday morning Ladies' Class in my childhood congregation (Wynne, Arkansas), though Pat had not lived there when I was growing up. When visiting my parents in Wynne once or twice a year I attended Pat's class. The first time I heard her pray, I looked up at her in amazement. She prayed as if she were talking to someone with whom she had a long and intimate acquaintance. It was beautiful.

Coming to know Jo and Pat caused me to begin to wonder if there were more to Christianity than believing the right things and doing the right things. These had always seemed adequate to me before, but they somehow seemed incomplete now. Around this time I saw a strange insurance advertisement on television which opened the eyes of my heart to a new truth. The advertisement dwelt for several long seconds on an unusual rendering of the Mona Lisa. As the camera panned closer to the famous face, I could see that it was actually a paint-by-number version of that great painting. It was, of course, quite ugly. The point of the advertisement was the value of authenticity or genuineness. In a moment of piercing insight I pictured myself as a paint-by-number Christ, not the real thing, with gentleness, faithfulness, love, joy, and peace painted on in little sections, on the outside of my skin. It was not an attractive picture. This was very disturbing to me, but I was unsure how to remedy it.

The pivotal event of my young adulthood happened after we had moved from Memphis to Iowa. In the fall of 1980 I began to have a few odd physical symptoms that didn't add up to much: I felt weak, somewhat listless; my cycle was a little irregular; something wasn't right. I went to the student health clinic at the University of Iowa. The doctor could find nothing, and intimated that my physical ailments were really psychosomatic. That disturbed me more than not feeling well. A week later I went to another doctor; he said perhaps it was the flu, and gave me some medicine.

A few days later, I nearly fainted on my way home from classes. I began to have lower abdominal pain, which increased hourly. Late in the evening I experienced a sharp pain, like a flower with talons opening up. After an initial exam at the emergency room, the student doctor was unable to diagnose the problem. The next morning it was discovered that I had an ectopic pregnancy (a pregnancy in the fallopian tube) which had ruptured the night before, and I had been bleeding internally since. I was whisked off to emergency surgery, where it was found that I had lost several pints of blood, and serious infection had set in. Recovery was long and devastating, physically, emotionally, as well as spiritually.

During the long months of recuperation I began to question God and the purpose and meaning of prayer. I spent a year studying all the prayers in the Bible. What I was looking for was whether God really loves and protects his own. I had believed that bad things couldn't happen to God's people. I had to change my theology or my category—and I didn't want to do either. The brothers and sisters in the church in Iowa City were very understanding with me. There were some in this church, too, like Jo and Pat, who saw things with spiritual eyes. I studied and learned, not exactly the direct answers to my questions, but something more valuable. I began to see scripture as something more than proof-text; it began to live.

Years of Re-Orientation
From Iowa we moved to Abilene, Texas where we had two babies in quick succession, and my questions receded awhile as I was buried in Martha kinds of duties for a couple of years. But a great thirst, a great hunger was developing in me. God sent more Jos and Pats into my life, and I listened and began to recognize that I wanted more of what they had, but did not know how to find it.

In my 30s I once again began attending a Ladies' Bible Class, this time at the University Church of Christ in Abilene. I was part of that group for three years. Near the end of that time I was asked to teach Galatians. I studied a whole summer for a four-class series, re-embarking on the journey I had begun a few years earlier in my quest to understand how bad things happen to good people. God's word became a new book. I realized I had been starving. I felt like someone who had been anemic for years who receives several pints of whole iron-rich red blood; like someone who had been closed in a small airless room for years who gets to go for a walk by the ocean. I, who had known all about Christianity, began to know what I had not known. I began to know my God.

Soon after this I joined a group of women who were studying the Bible inductively. This was a whole group of Jos and Pats. This was Camilla Becton's women's Bible study group at Highland in Abilene. First we studied Colossians, then we spent a year in John.

At this point several of us from the Minter Lane Church of Christ formed an evening Bible study group so that women who worked outside the home could join us. This group met for about ten years, with three of us (Melanie Savage, Carla McDonald, and I) as the core organizers. First we worked through a book called *Lord, I Want to Know You*, by Kay Arthur (Multnomah). It was during this study that I began to know God as my Jehovah Raapha (healer), El Elyon (God Most High or Sovereign), Jehovah Jireh (provider), Adonai (Lord), and Jehovah Tsidkenu (righteousness). Then we studied 1, 2, and 3 John, then Judges. One year we studied Ephesians, another Hebrews. Two years we studied Romans.

Though we took turns leading, in a sense we were simply learning together. But as those of us in our 30s began to enter our 40s, we realized that the women in their 20s were looking to us as the "older women" who were to teach the "younger women." We felt too young, but we accepted the challenge. It was a new and strange feeling.

We studied again the names of God and 1, 2, and 3 John. We wrote some of our own study material, following the inductive approach. For ten years this Bible study was the center of my life. It grounded me, taught me, anchored me, lifted me, changed my heart. I began to feel less like a paint-by-number Christ, more and more that I myself was being transformed, not just painted over.

The Legacy
The years in the Word have watered a deep well in me from which I have drawn for the various ministries God has given me over the years. My primary ministry in Churches of Christ has been with children. I

have also taught adults: women's classes and retreats as well as men and women in mission settings, lectureship classes, and seminars. More recently my ministry has included mentoring and comforting the broken as I have been comforted.

My secular work has been in the field of education; I have worked with public schools in Arkansas, Mississippi, Tennessee, Iowa, Texas, and California. I have also taught educational methods and theory courses at the university level. As I taught Sunday school and children's church over the last 30 years I imported exciting new educational methodologies and theories into the Bible school classroom (e.g., cooperative learning, learning centers, discovery method). These were years when developmental theory from education began to inundate the Christian Bible school market; I participated in that infusion, wholeheartedly applying secular methods in Christian settings.

About fifteen years ago I began to question the wholesale importation of secular educational methodology into Christian education. As I spent more time in the Word, I began to ask some questions: Are the goals of Christian religious instruction essentially the same as that of public school instruction, i.e., the passing on of basic skills and knowledge? What *are* the primary goals of Christian religious instruction? Are public school methods and approaches the best way to teach these goals?

The traditional Christian education goals of knowing (knowing about God), being (being like God), and doing (acting like God) inform the answer to these questions. Knowledge acquisition can be an important Sunday school goal (e.g., memory verses, Biblical chronology, stories of principal Bible characters) and many public school methods will work quite successfully in this arena. Teaching children to be like God and act like God will, however, require more than the typical public school model. For children to begin to be like God on the inside and act like him on the outside (something which we adults have yet to achieve) will entail their coming to know God. The question I began to ask was: How can teachers help children come to know God?

My quest to understand children's spirituality has run so deep that three years ago I began full-time doctoral work in Christian Education.

My dissertation focuses on children's spirituality. Last year I spoke at the first International Conference on Children's Spirituality in England. I also helped write a grant which will fund a conference in 2003 on children's spirituality, and I am currently working with others at Talbot School of Theology (Biola University, La Mirada, California) to found a Center for Children's Spirituality.

Thus far my study has convinced me even more that children must be taught from the Word, must spend time in the Word in order to get to know their Father. They must also spend time with those who know God and are seeking to be like him and act like him. As I began to write materials for children's Sunday school, I renewed my commitment to a biblical focus, incorporating contemporary educational methodology and principles as I wrote. I also sought ways to include experiences for children in intergenerational settings, since the children in biblical times learned in this manner. I have adapted some of the adult studies for children, e.g., the *Names of God* series, and have written other materials on Acts, the fruit of the Spirit, and the Exodus (*Wilderness Journey*, Touch Outreach, 1998). The ultimate purpose for each of the series is to grow children of faith; the focus is on coming to know God through time in the Word, prayer, and ministry in multi-age settings.

My grandmother's legacy has affected my ministry in other ways also. As I have taught adults over the years, I have sought to shape the studies in a way that the participants work together in small groups and dig the truths out of Scripture themselves. I also have attempted to bring the older and younger together. One Ladies' Day was attended by a third teens, a third women in their 30's and 40's, and a third older women. I have tended to focus primarily on biblical studies, not topical issues (e.g., how to be a good mother or a better financial manager). Though these are worthy topics, others have been called to those ministries. I believe it is time in the Word which nurtures relationship with God which in turn empowers a godly life. The how-to's are important but not sufficient—secondary, not primary.

The last area of ministry which has risen from the years in the Word has come about due to circumstances in my life. These past four years have again been years of disorientation for me. My family has experienced public losses and personal grief. We have lost some of the outward signs of stability and security—position in a community, a sense of place. Brothers and sisters whom we loved turned away from us. We felt abandoned.

My biblical heritage has provided the strength and anchor I have needed in this time of suffering and loss. Verses I memorized as a child have risen to lift my heart and encourage my spirit, e.g., "May the God of hope fill you with all joy and peace as you trust in him, so that you may overflow with hope by the power of the Holy Spirit" (Rom. 15:13, *NIV*). The word "hope" has new meaning in this place.

I have leaned upon promises learned long ago. I found a pillowcase with the following promises printed on it:

Our Thinking	*His Promise*
It's impossible.	All things are possible. (Luke 18:27)
I'm too tired.	I will give you rest. (Matt. 11:28-30
Nobody really loves me.	I love you. (John 3:16)
I can't go on.	My grace is sufficient. (2 Cor. 12:9)
I can't figure things out.	I will direct your steps. (Prov. 20:24)
I'm not able.	I am able. (2 Cor. 9:8)
It's not worth it.	It will be worth it. (Rom 8:28)
I can't forgive myself.	I forgive you. (1 John 1:9; Rom 8:1)
I can't manage.	I will supply all your need. (Phil. 4:19)
I'm afraid.	I have not given you a spirit of fear. (2 Tim. 1:7)
I'm always worried.	Cast all your care on me. (1 Pet. 5:7)
I haven't enough faith.	I've given everyone a measure of faith. (Rom. 12:8)
I'm not smart enough.	I give you wisdom. (1 Cor. 1:30)
I feel so alone.	I will never leave you or forsake you. (Heb. 13:5)

Many nights during the last four years I have slept on that pillowcase and read and re-read the promises and scriptures just before turning out the light.

I have recently completed a Bible study focusing primarily on Isaiah 61:1-4 (Beth Moore's *Breaking Free*, Lifeway Press). This study has been a healing balm for the wounds of recent years. Knowing that

Christ came "to bind up the broken-hearted" (Isaiah 61: 1b), "to comfort those who mourn" (v. 2b), and "to provide for those who grieve" (v. 3a) has comforted me immensely. And I anticipate the day when He will "bestow ... a crown of beauty instead of ashes, the oil of gladness instead of mourning, and a garment of praise instead of a spirit of despair" (v. 3b). And I long to be an "oak of righteousness, a planting of the Lord for the display of *his* splendor" (v. 3b).

As a result of this difficult time God has opened the eyes of my heart to other broken and hurting people, an insight which has led to my "pillowcase" ministry. I have given the "Promises" pillowcase to women whose husbands have been diagnosed with cancer, a mother whose children are in rebellion, a woman whose husband was lost in the World Trade Center, and a mother who deals daily with a child with cerebral palsy. Before 1997 I taught *about* God's healing power, his mercy, his desire to empower us to forgive; now I have experienced these things. I *know* them in the *yada* sense of the word. This kind of knowledge speaks in a way nothing else can.

The Larger Legacy
When I think of the subtitle of this book, *The Way of Women in Churches of Christ*, I think of the hundreds and thousands of Ladies' Bible Classes that have met faithfully for decades across the last century. I think of the women, like my grandmother, who have been daily in the Word.

Not to say that men have not been in the Word; they have. It was from men that I originally learned what I believe and why I believe it—from men in the pulpit and college Bible classes. From these men I learned a tremendous amount about theology, church history, and apologetics. Much of what I learned is important for a well-grounded faith. But for me it was from the women with whom I studied that I learned how to live that faith.

The legacy from my grandmother—time daily in the Word—is not a legacy exclusively from my grandmother. It is a legacy of Churches of Christ everywhere. We have been people of the Book. It is surely one of the greatest legacies a church could pass on. The habit of daily time in the Word has empowered my ministry to children, undergirded my teaching to adults, enabled my ministry to broken people, and sustained my life. How profoundly grateful I am to have been among Christians grounded in the Word, committed to study.

I was 25 years old when Dorothy Simpson shared with me her desire for heaven. That was a quarter of a century ago. I am approaching 50, close to my grandmother's age when I spent those summers with her. My grandmother went to be with her Lord when she was 75. I wonder if I will have another 25 years to grow and learn and teach as did my grandmother. I do not know what other work God has in store for me. In the meantime I will continue the work he has given me to do: mentoring younger women, teaching as I am called, and researching and writing about children's spirituality.

My dear daughter-in-law is expecting to give birth to our first grandchild in a few months. I hope this grandchild may have the opportunity to visit me in the summers so that I can share with her (or him) what God has taught me. I hope to play Candy Land or Uno with this child, water the pansies together, and sit on my blue couch studying the Word with this dear grandchild nearby. It is the fondest dream of my life that I may pass on to my children and their children the legacy my grandmother bestowed upon me.

I do not know if the work God has given me to do is over. I am content to stay and do whatever else he has in mind. But I also am content to go.

Note

[1]My grandmother was Dessie Imboden (1903-1979) of Hickory Ridge, Arkansas.

Holly Catterton Allen lives in Orange, California with her husband, Leonard Allen. They have two adult sons and one teenage daughter.

Holly is nearing completion of a Ph.D. in Christian Education at Talbot School of Theology, Biola University, La Mirada, California.

She also teaches as an adjunct professor at Biola University; speaks at seminars, retreats and professional conferences; and writes for professional and devotional publications.

8

The Accidental Ministry

Anita Johnson

My sweet young friend sat across the table from me, sipping now and then from her coffee cup, her eyes shining with joy and peace. "I just asked the Lord to show me the way, and he did. I know this path is the one my Father wants me to follow because the answer was so clear."

I returned her smile and murmured sounds of encouragement. I took a sip of my coffee to hide my own emotions. Why does this not happen to me? Why don't I hear God's voice directing me on the road he wants me to take? I didn't doubt that this friend had, indeed, heard the voice of God. She, like many other of my friends, walks her road of service with confidence that she is doing exactly what God wants her to do. Why am I so lacking?

Let me be clear. I am not talking about choices between what is sin and what is involved in holy living before our Lord. I am speaking of the many roads we take that are choices between good and better.

After over 50 years as a Christian, I can say that I have rarely known what it was that my Lord wanted me to do in my life. My Christian walk seems similar to the rest of my life. I bump into things. I lose car keys. I forget appointments. In other words, I am a klutz. How can God use a person like me? Yet I affirm that he can and has used me. As Paul wrote in 2 Corinthians 12:9: "But he said to me, 'My grace is sufficient for you, for my power is made perfect in weakness.'" If that is the case, I may be very good at demonstrating what God can do in a non-descript person's life. Perhaps this is what J. R. R. Tolkien was saying when he called Bilbo Baggins "a humble hero (blessed with a little wisdom and a little courage and considerable good luck)."

Choices must be made about how I spend my time and energy. The former seems to be increasing as the latter wanes. Where does God want me to live? Which request for money is the most important? How can I best use the gifts he has given me? I could really use a personal letter, a telephone call or an e-mail from God pointing the way.

In spite of the fact that I have fumbled and wandered these past 50 years, I will testify that God has used me, often in ways I didn't expect, probably in ways I never suspected, and always in spite of my own efforts and weakness. I think of my ministries as accidental ministries. While I was going one direction, God placed in my path something he wanted me to do, and I had to do it before I could move on. The perfect example of this was the fifteen years of care I gave my parents, the book which came from it, and the ministry I have of helping other eldercare givers. But I get ahead of my story.

Learning about Grace

I grew up in Southern California in a small Arkansas church. Most of the members were not only from Arkansas but from the same county, Madison. Many were related. The preacher who made the largest impact on me was Weldon Bennett, a Texan who graduated from Abilene Christian College. Brother Bennett baptized me at the age of 10, and I remember thinking, "Now that I have given my life to Jesus, I must stop lying." I was an intense and sincere little Christian.

Preachers didn't stay in one place very long those days, and after Brother Bennett left we had a series of preachers who were less well educated and less "mainstream" than he had been. Gradually our congregation drifted, or was led into a—how shall I say—non-cooperative, anti- (I don't like that term), legalistic position. With no other frame of reference, my husband and I accepted this position. As the town grew and new folks moved into the area, many were discontented with the kind of church we had become. When they started a new congregation across town, we stayed with the old group, a decision we both deeply regret.

Legalistic churches are not good places to raise children. When our teenage son agonized over whether he could serve in the military and if so, if he should go to Vietnam, while the Civil Rights movement was exposing abuses perpetuated towards black citizens, our congregation was arguing about whether we could have a baby shower in the building. Our son left for college and never darkened the door of a Church of Christ again.

Finally we went over to the other group, and I learned about grace—a wonderful experience for this little legalist who felt compelled to watch herself and others for any sign of law breaking. One especially embarrassing incident that happened before my enlightenment was my attitude toward one of the women in the congregation who never attended church on Sunday night. She was a hairdresser, and I made an appointment for a haircut with the intention of "tactfully" encouraging her to quit her sinful custom of missing Sunday night services.

While cutting my hair, Johnny related that she was so tired on Saturday night after a long day on her feet in the shop, she could barely get to church on Sunday morning. But by Mondays, her day off, she was rested enough to go to a nearby nursing home to cut and fix the residents' hair for free. She related that she clipped finger and toe nails and wiped the dust off the wheels of their wheelchairs. Even my legalistic little heart could see that this woman knew something about serving God that I had somehow missed. I accidentally got a glimpse of true Christianity, and was thankful the words I had planned to say went unsaid.

Learning about the grace of God was the most freeing thing I ever experienced as a Christian. Without a checklist of things to do to keep from going to hell, I was eager to find my gifts and joyfully serve such a wonderful Father who accepted and loved me unconditionally.

Growing through Serving and Teaching

Our years at the Sunny Hills Church of Christ were a rich time of growth. We had godly friends, good Bible teaching and opportunities to serve. My husband, Courtland, who has a tender heart and a generous nature, seemed bent on solving the homeless problem in our community. They could all come to our house to live. I won't attempt to share all the problems this caused. Suffice it to say, some homeless people are homeless because they do drugs and/or don't want to work. Naturally, they took advantage of us. While I was torn between resentment for being taken advantage of and reluctance to thwart Courtland's perceived ministry, we received a call from Ralph Beck at the Long Beach church. Ralph said that a battered mother, a member of their congregation, had sought help from the elders. They offered to put her up in a motel, but she requested to be allowed to live with a Christian family for awhile. Ralph said they didn't want her with a family from their congregation for fear her husband would find her. Could he bring her and her children to stay with us?

I can truly say this was a most rewarding experience. With a spirit of forgiveness that I had never experienced, she would ask us to pray for her husband. My attitude was that any man who hits his wife should have various body parts cut off and fed to the vultures, so her sweet, forgiving spirit was a further lesson to me about the grace of God.

When she and her children left, she knew that she would accept no more abuse, and we knew that opening our home was a good ministry. We just needed to be more selective about who we invited in.

Shortly after this incident, I was invited to partner with four other women in a home Bible study. Each of us was to bring an unchurched friend, and when our turn came, prepare a Bible lesson from our own experiences that would confront, convict and challenge. I was so excited. The four other women were friends I admired greatly. I was flattered to be a part of such a talented group. I was amazed to see how the lessons presented captivated our unchurched group. One lady confessed that when she started coming, she wasn't sure she even believed in God. The impact of the word of God left no doubt in her mind that God is.

When my turn came to present the lesson, I was really bad. I had studied hard and felt I had something to say, but I had no idea how to organize it into a meaningful lesson. My previous efforts at teaching were with children, and I had a lesson book that organized the material for me. My sisters were not critical, but I knew how bad I was. The second time my turn came I was no better. On my knees I implored the Father to help me learn to teach, or tell me I should quit the group. Help came from my husband, who is a natural teacher, and from David Skates who, as our preacher, taught a class on preparing a Bible class lesson.

I was feeling pretty good. I had always loved studying the Bible, and now it seemed that God had given me the gift of teaching and wanted to use me in that way. I knew the road I should follow.

Questioning Traditions

It was during this time that I began to question the traditional views of the way women can serve in our assemblies. An appeal was made for ushers. We were told that Deacon Larry was having trouble finding ushers. Our congregation was growing, partly due to our ladies' class, and it was important for those who didn't arrive early to have help finding a seat. The job seemed earmarked for me. With my new-found confidence, my pride in my friendly manner, and my eagle eye for a vacant seat, I called Deacon Larry's house and volunteered. There was a long, uncomfortable silence. Than a voice said, "Well, (cough) you know the ushers help pass the communion at the back."

Suddenly my lifetime acceptance of our fellowship's custom that only men could walk up and down the aisles with the communion trays hit the light of reason. I suppressed a hysterical giggle. This conversation was ridiculous, should not be happening. Knowing I wasn't going to change anything, my perverse nature caused me to play dumb.

"I think I can handle that job. I have been passing the communion trays for years. True, I have usually been seated while doing so, but on occasion, when the person down the aisle was too far away, I have been known to rise and walk down the aisle. Truthfully, I probably crouched while doing this. If I passed the communion in a

crouching position, would I be able to help at the back of the auditorium?"

The questions of how this custom got started began to gnaw at
me. Then I remembered that, early in our marriage, my young husband was invited to attend a leadership class at church. Even in my
unlearned state, I had some idea that learning leadership methods was
pretty sophisticated stuff and I wondered what our elders and our current preacher knew about teaching such a class. My curiosity was satisfied when my husband returned home.

He grinned at me and said, "We learned that when we 'wait on
the table' we should wear a coat and tie."

Now, years later, the communion passing restriction on women was
explained. Passing the communion trays is a leadership activity forbidden to women. I acquiesced. The congregation lost a friendly, charming usher, and I had a new frame for one of our fellowship's customs.

Today, as the debate has been joined about the roles women can
fill in the public assembly, I still hear the term "leadership" used. This,
from educated men who should be able to distinguish between leadership and service. I think women can provide leadership, too, but
what happens in our assemblies doesn't have much to do with leadership. When we get the language changed to "serving" in our assemblies, we can more easily move past this artificial barrier.

Closing Doors

It was mid-August of 1978, and a good time in my life. Doors seemed
to be opening for me that offered a promise that I could fulfill some
cherished dreams. My children were all out of the house so I was
freed of being a hands-on parent. Our business was doing well, and
we had some high-quality employees, so I was freed from long hours
at work. With my newfound confidence that God wanted me to be a
teacher, I prepared to finish my bachelor's degree at a local Bible college. I knew what I wanted to do, and I was sure this was the road
God wanted me to take.

In the registrar's office I was warned that employment opportunities would be very limited for me in any church of Christ. I was not

discouraged. Things were changing, and I felt confident that if this were the road God wanted me to take, he would take care of any roadblocks.

Returning to my office, I came face to face with a challenge that would take me down a very different road for the next 15 years. My dad had returned from his annual summer in the Rockies, and something was very wrong with him.

Caring for first my father and then my mother was a "no contest" decision. My brother Gene and I were it. Our parents, though divorced from each other, were devoted parents. We loved them. We had to do what had to be done.

We joined the ranks of adults who provide care to elderly relatives. The *Wall Street Journal* has stated that more working days are lost to eldercare than to childcare. There is a myth that has been around for a long time that Americans don't take good care of their elderly parents. This is wrong. Americans are no different from any other group of people. We love and care for our elderly parents.

Gene and I compared notes with friends who were in the same situation. We looked for information. We made mistakes. We grieved the losses Daddy was experiencing as his mind no longer enabled him to be the freedom-loving adventurer he had always been

Grief was the hardest part of the experience. I ranted at God for allowing this to happen in my father. I questioned that he would cut short, before it even began, my brilliant college career, because the time I spent with Dad was consuming the time I could spend away from our business.

When, after three years, Dad died, our mother's health had begun declining. Then the cruelest blow of all, my brother, who was my friend and constant helper, died.

My mother's health worsened, and three times the summer following Gene's death, I had to move her to a higher level of care. The heavy moving stuff had always been Gene's job. Using his truck and any young man I could rope in, I moved her. Each time I called to the heavens to send my brother back to be my friend and do the work I wasn't physically or mentally equipped to do.

I couldn't understand why God had put me where he had. I didn't want to do these things. I didn't know how to handle most of the tasks that came my way. I had other responsibilities, too, besides our business. Our youngest daughter had a pregnancy that demanded full bedrest, so we were caring for her and her toddler since her husband had bailed out of the marriage. There were other family challenges, and there were many times when I felt I was going down for the third time. Some dear sister would remind me that God never gives us more than we can bear. I was always tempted to state that God had badly overestimated what I could bear.

I became very familiar with the book of Job during this time as I tried to hold on to some kind of reason and sanity. Additionally, the Psalms were a comfort, as well as wonderful book by Henry Gariepy called *Portraits of Perseverance: 100 Meditations from the Book of Job*.

I learned to accept the fact that I might never understand why God had given me this task. Accepting where I was was harder. In *Portraits of Perseverance*, I came upon a piece that spoke to me:

> Only in acceptance lies peace, not in resignation
>   nor in busyness.
> Resignation is surrender to fate
> Acceptance is surrender to God.
> Resignation lies down quietly in an empty universe.
> Acceptance rises up to meet the God who fills that
>   universe with purpose and destiny.
> Resignation says, "I can't."
> Acceptance says, "God can!"
> Resignation says, "What a waste."
> Acceptance asks, "In what redemptive way will
>   you use this mess, Lord?"[1]

I confess that I still have not learned the lesson of acceptance, but at least I know now that I need to.

On December 6, 1994, while we sat in a hospital waiting the results of our son-in-law's spinal cancer surgery, I received a phone call that Mom had died. We knew she was close to death when we left, but when I asked her permission to go be with our oldest daughter, Gail, she indicated her wish that we leave. I really thought I would get back before Mom died, but that was not to be. Another of those unanswered questions.

Helping Other Caregivers
Believing that God has a purpose for every life we place in his hands, even mine, and believing that God wastes nothing, I wondered how others could benefit from all the mistakes I had made, as well as the lessons I had learned. A book! I would write a book. In the book I would talk about the wild emotional swings the adult child experiences as we go from trying to fix all that is wrong in our parent's life to resenting the sacrifices caregiving demands in our own lives. I would share creative solutions that my friends and I had found for some caregiving challenges.

I had never had any training to write, didn't understand our word processor very well, and can't spell. There is no need to remind me that word processors correct spelling. You still have to get close to the correct spelling for the spell check to work. I can't tell you how many times my computer has said, "I have no idea what you are trying to write. Are you attempting to communicate in English?'

In spite of my limitations, the book *Sunset Decisions* was written, and a publisher was found. Again my ministry was clear. This masterpiece of helpful information would go forth, blessing thousands of heartsick caregivers with new information and hope. It hasn't quite worked that way. I hope the book has blessed the few hundreds of people who have bought it, but thousands? Hardly. A sweet ministry, but not, numerically at least, an impressive one.

Additionally, I offered my information to churches for seminars. Before I used up all the close friends and relatives who invited me to give a seminar, I had collected lots of additional information. The seminars were getting better and better, but churches were not beating a path to my door.

My most recent seminar was a four-hour event in Austin, Texas. Terry Thomley, the education director, did a good job of advertising it, and it was well attended. The next evening, while we debriefed, Terry asked me, "Anita, what are you doing to promote this seminar? These attendees gave you their attention for four hours. This tells me that you have information that caregivers need. There is nothing else like this being offered, as far as I know. You need to get the word out so other churches will invite you."

Terry is a kind man and had no intention of putting a guilt trip on me, but I returned home feeling that I had failed by not doing a better job of promoting the seminar. How many hundreds of people who needed the seminar were denied the opportunity of attending due to my lack of marketing skill?

Then my cousin, Linda Beck, reminded me that this may not be the ministry that God has for me, or else I have already helped the people God had for me to help. She said that my job was to be prepared and available and trust that God would do with me what he wanted.

I remembered a few people I had met whom I knew I had truly helped. There was the lady who said, "I thought I was going crazy until I came here and learned that most caregivers feel these emotions."

I remembered the lady in Maryland who was clearly in burnout because her very angry mother-in-law was living in her home and beating her up emotionally because she wanted to return to her own home. Her friend called me after the seminar and said they had intervened with the husband and persuaded him to place his parents in a retirement facility.

A man in California told me he had been planning to move his mother from the Midwest to California until my seminar, when I encouraged caregivers to consider what a parent will have to give up by moving from his or her home.

Was it possible that I had done what God wanted me to do? After all, Jesus spent an afternoon with one lady beside a well in Sychar, and he had only three years in which to do all he had to do in his earthly body. Surely, I shouldn't measure my ministry by numbers.

Again I had to be reminded that, while I go one direction, God likely has other plans for me. That he has been able to use me at all is amazing. For the times he has used me, I feel humbly grateful. What a testimony to a great God who can use the scared, mud-drenched foot soldier in his mighty army. What a testimony that he can use a klutz like me.

So now, when a friend glowingly relates the guidance she is receiving from our Lord, I smile and commend her. I am happy God has given her a road map. I am doing fine without a road map, because I have figured out that I am not driving.

Notes

1. Quoted in Creath Davis, *Lord if I Ever Needed You* (Baker).
2. *Sunset Decisions* (Joplin, MO: College Press).

Anita M. Johnson lives in Salinas, California with her husband Courtland, a retired CPA. They have three children and two grandchildren.

For many years, they worked together in Courtland's accounting firm. Since 1998 Anita has been writing. She has published one book, *Sunset Decisions*, and several articles. She has recently completed an as-yet-unpublished novel, *Scent of Pines*.

The Johnsons are part of a house church.

9

An 'Act of Worship'

Geannetta Bennett

Therefore, I urge you, brothers, in view of God's mercy,
to offer your bodies as living sacrifices, holy and pleasing to God
—this is your spiritual act of worship. (Rom. 12:1)

I remember sitting in my bedroom, trying desperately to come to grips with the decision I had made. "Maybe it's time to give up this child-hood fantasy of acting—time to grow up and seek to serve in a more meaningful way. After all, who can honestly say that what you have is a gift?"

My heart sank as if someone had died. There was the familiar lump in my throat, the one that always appears when I try to confine myself to standards I have adopted but am not convicted of. I have held this dream in my heart since I was a child. Though everything about me has changed, this dream has remained constant—the dream of sharing the expressions of my heart with my Lord and Master through drama and song. How could I silence the words and melodies that danced around in my head? How could I lay to rest this part of me that God has used all these years to sustain me, that made me uniquely Geannetta?

I cried in my room like a woman mourning a lost loved one as I laid my gift on a sacrificial altar made by my own hands. I waited for someone to comfort me or stop me, but everyone I discussed it with agreed it was time to move on. Just when I thought I was ready to dismiss this infantile preoccupation, a thought rushed into my head: "Who am I to deny God the one thing I do well? Who am I to tell God that his gift would not be used?"

My answer was not to sacrifice my gift, but to place it under submission as a tool of his service. Not to be used when and where I want, but when and where God chooses. Just because it hasn't been done doesn't mean it shouldn't be done. And just because it can't be a part of the formal worship service doesn't mean it can't be an act of worship.

An 'Act of Worship'

As a Christian performing artist, I write and present dramatic readings and songs at church-sponsored events and in community and cultural programs. As I do this, I must constantly examine the integrity of my performance. It's easy to get caught up in the process of performing and lose spiritual consciousness. To belabor an emotion or over-dramatize a character alienates the audience and subverts the concept of the piece. The audience senses the insincerity and dismisses the performance as trite and hypocritical. Offering myself should never be used as an occasion to call attention to myself. It is a sacrifice.

Christian theater should be used to link scriptural concepts and personal application. Not to teach theology or doctrine, but to illustrate the principles taught. Art in its various forms has always been used to provoke the observer to consider more than the obvious. Art forms are not created to tell the patron what to think, only that he or she should think. Christian artists must remain true to their artistic expression as a gift from God to be shared, not a truth revealed. If we misunderstand our position in using such a gift, we cease being artists and become "soothsayers."

A Christian artist may be drawn in by the applause and accolades. The bright lights and the stage satisfy a need in many of us to perform, but is that the goal of the performance? If we limit ourselves to this form of praise, what reward is left us from the Father? Matthew warns us not to be deceived by one of Satan's most powerful devices, the trap of confining ourselves to the praise of men. "Be careful not to do your 'acts of righteousness' before men, to be seen by them. If you do, you will have no reward from your Father in heaven" (Matt. 6:1).

We should aspire to loftier heights than the temporal pleasures of this world. Our goal should be spiritual gains, not carnal pleasures. All praise belongs to God, and the job of the Christian performer is to evoke praise for him, not for ourselves. As servants of Christ, we have been entrusted with a precious gift. This gift must be used to invite souls to experience an intimate relationship with God. Although we embody the talent, we are often unaware of its magnitude. It is not the actor who persuades people to be saved, but the gospel within the dramatic performance. If we do not use this gift to direct people to Christ, of what use is it? It is only useful when we yield our way to God's will and allow others to see the power of God's Word.

Only God can decide how and when to use us as Christian artists. Being driven people who think and move rapidly, we must resist the urge to act impulsively or emotionally in our desire to share our gifts. Even though we may feel equipped to perform certain functions because of our God-given abilities, we must ask ourselves whether it is God's desire, especially for those of us who are women. Think of it this way: The King requests what he wants and whom he wants to "act" in his royal court. Performers who were not pleasing to the King have been put to death for their acts before him. "Aaron's sons Nadab and Abihu took their censers, put fire in them and added incense; and they offered unauthorized fire before the Lord, contrary to his command. So fire came out from the presence of the Lord and consumed them, and they died before the Lord" (Lev. 10:1, 2).

Our gifts were given to edify the church and glorify God. The thoughts we impress upon our audience will be taken seriously, even literally. If an idea is still in its infancy, we must wait for it to develop clearly and make sure we can live with it comfortably. Artistic expression does not absolve us of the responsibility to seek the best interests of the body of Christ.

As a Christian artist, I am accountable for what I express to an audience, just as any other Christian is accountable in presenting his or her gift. "So it is with you. Since you are eager to have spiritual gifts, try to excel in gifts that build up the church" (1 Cor. 14:12). The overall purpose for using our gifts is to glorify God. If the gift does not bring glory to God, it is not an act of worship, but an act meant to call attention to ourselves.

William Jones of Memphis, Tennessee says, "Worship is not worship until we realize we have no right to be there." Worshipping God is a privilege and an honor. Being part of the family of God is not the same as being part of a democratic society where every citizen has a say in how things are done. God is a loving Father, and we are his children. Our job is to trust and obey, not tell the Creator what should or should not be done to honor him. Many of us as artists behave like spoiled children, demanding to have our "fair share," stomping our feet with wind in our cheeks because our gifts are not being honored in the worship service as are those of others. So we resort to doing one of several things: We take on tasks we are not especially skilled to perform. We become critical of those performing tasks we feel qualified to perform ourselves. We condemn the church for being ineffective, limited, and unproductive because we aren't allowed to use our gifts in the worship. In many cases, we bury our gift.

Worship is not about us. Our gifts may be creative, innovative and thought-provoking. But not all gifts are appropriate for the worship service of the King. A Christian artist with gifts given by God will not realize the true potential of those gifts until they are totally surrendered to the Lord's service. Our Father, knowing us so intimately, has designed each of us for a task. He has empowered us with a unique talent to perform the job created for us. Yielding these abilities to his wisdom will only increase our blessings. If we possess a gift God wants used in the worship service, it is our duty to use that gift with all that is within us. However, if that gift is one that cannot be used in the worship service, it is our responsibility to search for a means by which the gift can be used to glorify God. If we withhold the gift because it is not proper in a worship service, we are no better than the one-talent servant.

> "Again, it will be like a man going on a journey, who called his servants and entrusted his property to them. To one he gave five talents of money, to another two talents, and to another one talent, each according to his ability. Then he went on his journey. The man who had received the five talents went at once and put his money to work and gained five more. So also, the one with the two talents gained two more. But the man who had received the one talent went off, dug a hole in the ground and hid his master's money" (Matt. 25:14-18).

God has entrusted us with gifts to use to his glory, so we may present him with abundance in the last day. To question his wisdom is not only foolish, but dangerous. We will have to answer for what we've done with what has been entrusted to us. The one-talent servant was under the misconception that if he simply gave back to his master what had been given to him, he would owe nothing. Not only was he mistaken in the debt he owed, but he was punished for being "lazy" and not investigating other options in seeking a return on the talent given him.

> "His master replied, 'You wicked, lazy servant! So you knew that I harvest where I have not sown and gather where I have not scattered seed? Well then, you should have put my money on deposit with the bankers, so that when I returned I would have received it back with interest.
> "'Take the talent from him and give it to the one who has the ten talents. For everyone who has will be given more, and he will have an abundance. Whoever does not have, even what he has will be taken from him. And throw that worthless servant outside, into the darkness, where there will be weeping and gnashing of teeth'" (Matt. 25:26-30).

As a Christian performing artist, I must trust my Father. Like an eager child with a beautiful art project, I rush to my Father's house ready to share. I hold my gift up with a big smile, expecting a warm reception, and when it doesn't come, I'm hurt. God isn't telling me that he doesn't appreciate my gift. Of course he does. He gave it to me! I present my gift to him proudly proclaiming, "See what I made for you, Daddy? Can we hang it on the door for everyone to see when they come into the house?" Our loving Father says, "No, my child. I have something very important on the door that everyone must see when they enter, so they will know this house belongs to me." Then he gently guides me to another location and says, "Not there, but here. This way I can look at your gift every day and smile at what you have done."

Doesn't that feel better? Knowing that God has not prohibited the artist's gifts from the worship, but has given us the vehicle of art by which we are given liberty to praise him. When we consider all the possibilities for sharing the gospel by means of the arts, we're overwhelmed. There are situations in which a Bible class would be inappropriate, but a dramatic presentation of a biblical personality would be welcome. Prayer and subject matter pertaining to religion is taboo in our public schools, but a spiritual song giving praise to God is regarded as cultural. As Paul did, we must use every opportunity afforded us as citizens of this country. "I am a Jew, from Tarsus in Cilicia, a citizen of no ordinary city. Please let me speak to the people" (Acts 21:39).

We must not consider ourselves restricted, but free. Free to express ourselves in ways that others cannot and to share the most indescribable gift, Christ Jesus, through the artistic gift God has entrusted to us. Such a paradigm shift can only occur when we understand that our worship is not limited to Sunday morning and the church building. We are the temples of God. We live a life of praise. Everything we do as a new creation, no longer belonging to us but to him who purchased us with his blood, is an act of worship. "Do you not know that your body is a temple of the Holy Spirit, who is in you, whom you have received from God? You are not your own; you were bought at a price. Therefore honor God with your body" (1 Cor. 6:19, 20).

My Alabaster Box

Once we have submitted our gift to the Father, there is yet another obstacle to contend with. Not everyone will esteem our efforts as noble. The Christian artist must expect to be challenged on the integrity and the necessity of a drama or music ministry. Some may consider the very notion unscriptural and unacceptable. There was a woman in scripture whose gift to Jesus was not considered acceptable by those who witnessed her offering (Lk. 7:36). But it did not stop her from pouring out her gift on him in a gesture of love that moved the Master and stands as a testimony for generations to come. "I tell you the truth, wherever this gospel is preached throughout the world, what she has done will also be told, in memory of her" (Matt. 26:13).

Drama is not a traditional arena of service, and not everyone will embrace it, but it is an act of worship, not an act of selfishness. We must be firm in our belief that in performing we are presenting our best gifts. We must be so driven by the love we have for the Lord that minor obstacles won't impede our service. The sinful woman was not saved by her gift of love, but by her faith. Our artistic ministries won't save us, only what we have done with what has been placed in our hands. Whether our gift is appreciated should not hinder us from proclaiming the gospel through the arts. We should move forward by faith, asking God's guidance throughout the entire creative process. When confronted by those who do not understand your gift, rest assured that God does and will judge, not on the perfection of the project, but on the faith with which it is presented.

Some audience members have commented after a performance that they would like to begin a drama ministry in their congregations. However, I'm not sure they understand the entire package. Being a Christian performer is a labor of love. Planning for a performance or presentation demands contemplation, prayer, study and tears. Sometimes the process leads to joy and learning and a sense of being attuned with God. I often rejoice over the work of the Holy Spirit and praise God for making his Word alive to me. At other times, the process is painful and humbling. I feel unworthy and can see where I have fallen short. I recall my past transgressions and wonder how God can use a woman like me. I am acutely aware of my idiosyncrasies, and Satan takes advantage of them. Almost without fail, when I prepare a presentation based on a principle I am developing in my personal life, I am tested on that principle. But thanks be to God, during these trials I am empowered and given not only the strength to endure, but an example of the principle in application. "Consider it pure joy, my brothers, whenever you face trials of many kinds, because you know that the testing of your faith develops perseverance. Perseverance must finish its work so that you may be mature and complete, not lacking anything" (James 1:2-4).

In that painful and humbling experience, I am drawn closer to God and made more complete. I want to pour out my gift like oil, and I am in tears while writing the lesson. I am totally submitted as an instrument of God, and through my tears, I rejoice.

I admire the sinful woman in Luke, not only because of her outpouring of love, but her courage in confronting her fears and the opponents who stand between her and Jesus. Nothing was more important than reaching Jesus and giving him her best. It wasn't the excellence of her offering, but her desire to be forgiven of the sin in her life that mattered. She was prepared to give her utmost and pledge her allegiance to a Savior worthy of praise.

I can understand how forgiveness can open a floodgate of tears. I can understand how unconditional love can be so overwhelming that I fall to my knees in praise. Understanding the magnitude of the gift of forgiveness, she washed his feet with her tears and covered them with kisses. One of the definitions of worship is "a kiss toward God." I want my dramatic performances to be just that—a kiss toward God.

The Ministry of Womanhood
Likewise, teach the older women to be reverent in the way they live, not to be slanderers or addicted to much wine, but to teach what is good. Then they can train the younger women to love their husbands and children, to be self-controlled and pure, to be busy at home, to be kind, and to be subject to their husbands, so that no one will malign the word of God (Titus 2:3-5).

There are some things that only a woman can teach another woman. I studied the powerful women in scripture for example and guidance. I wasn't particularly interested in creating dramatic presentations at the time. Then one evening, my sister Errica called me to sing a song she had written entitled, "The Master Plan." It was a beautiful depiction of Mary, the mother of Jesus, accepting the will of God in her son's crucifixion.

I began to think how Mary, like any mother, might have reflected on her son as a child and a young man as she witnessed his final moments. Any mother in that position would feel indescribable pain, and the only way to alleviate that pain would be to see a grander scheme at work. What faith and courage it must have taken to find clarity in the face of such tragedy. What magnificence she must have beheld as the sky darkened and the earth shook at her son's last breath; after all the cruelty and abuse, to tremble in his shadow and have it finally be so clear. That was when I began to write my performance piece "My Son, My Savior."

John describes a moment at the foot of the cross in words that transform in the mind like a developing photograph: "When Jesus saw his mother there, and the disciple whom he loved standing nearby, he said to his mother, 'Dear woman, here is your son,' and to the disciple, 'Here is your mother.' From that time on, this disciple took her into his home" (John 19:26, 27). It is a picture of the relationship between a mother and a son in its final and most painful transition. Jesus as the eldest son must perform his final responsibility as a human being, seeing to the care of his mother. Mary stands helpless, her power as a mother exhausted. As she witnesses the power of his majesty unfold before her eyes, her son becomes her Savior.

The emotions of the passage painted images in my mind, and the piece developed on its own. It was truly a gift, for once I began writing, I didn't stop until it was finished. I give God the glory and thank him for the Spirit working with me through his word. Since I first read this piece aloud, it has never failed to receive a response that glorifies God, and for that I am grateful. Since then, I have written many other pieces portraying women in scripture. Each has been a powerful lesson

and continues to bless my life in application as well as dramatic interpretation.

I began sharing these pieces at what our congregation calls
"Friends and Family Fellowship," a fifth Sunday fellowship program.
These programs provide a platform for church members to share their
talents in the performing arts and invite friends and family to the performance. The fellowship takes place after morning worship and a
lunch provided by the church. At the conclusion of the program, we
dismiss for evening worship.

A program like this accomplishes many goals. It provides an
opportunity for church members to share gifts that may not ordinari-
ly be shared. It alleviates some of the frustrations experienced by
Christian performing artists and allows them to edify the church family. It is a platform to allow young performers to hone their talents and
be encouraged to use their talents for the Lord. It brings friends and
family into the church building for a less intimidating gathering than
the worship service. When used properly, it can be a powerful evangelistic tool. Sometimes God can use a song or a poem to soften a
heart just enough to receive the seed of the gospel. Finally, it provides
an opportunity to discuss with visitors the difference between the
worship service and fellowship. These fellowships showcase the gifts
of the body of Christ and are quite entertaining. However, during worship, God is the only one in the "spotlight." The worship service is a
sacred event where God is the center of attention and we empty ourselves to honor him.

These programs were so well received we began presenting an
annual New Year's Eve play. These are generally one-act plays reflect-
ing the events of the previous year, attributes to encourage or discour-
age, or fictional stories with spiritual lessons. The plays range from
comedies to poignant dramas. For the past three years, attendance during the New Year's Eve program has increased. It's another opportunity to share the gospel through entertainment with the visitors the occasion attracts. The holidays are a wonderful time to reach out to the
community. Most people are in a festive mood, and those considering
a life change are more serious about it during this time of year.

The most powerful responses these dramatic lessons have received have been during ladies' day programs and retreats. During one season, there was a cast member from our congregation who was not a Christian. At the time, it didn't occur to me that she wasn't. The part she was given spoke indirectly to her situation. With encouragement and Bible classes taught by friends, she was baptized the Sunday following the performance. She was not converted by the play, but it prepared the soil for the seed. Through the nurture and camaraderie of being a cast member, our friend became a part of a network of love and support that did not end with the project.

Within this ministry, many victories have been won in the name of Jesus. Women struggling with the loss of a child have found comfort in Jochebed's story, "The Strength to Let Go." Many have connected with the human attributes of Bible personalities and have been encouraged to move forward in the name of the Lord. It's not the power of the drama, but the power of the gospel in the drama.

A woman telling a woman's story in a way only a woman can illuminates the truth and brings honor to God. What an effective tool this ministry can be! And this is only the beginning of the possibilities. For years, we have used puppet shows and short skits, but many other avenues should be investigated. I have stood in auditoriums of public schools and testified to the student body that "Jesus Is All Right," through the vehicle of song. Through storytelling and poetry readings in schools, libraries, and community centers, I have praised the Lord without fear of persecution. The opportunities are there, and the fields are ready for the harvest, if we only use the resources entrusted to us.

We women have a responsibility to each other. Who can teach a woman how to love her husband beyond the superficial way demonstrated in the media? Who can teach our young women the confidence and spiritual integrity they need to survive in an immoral society? Our young girls have been overwhelmed by images of scantily dressed women screaming their independence. Only we are equipped to instruct and empower. Only another woman can explain the liberation of submission and the opportunities that await us when we reconcile ourselves to the mission given to us and only us in the word of God.

Submission is not a subservient position, but one of power. God endows people with the wealth of his wisdom through paradox. To be strong we must first be made weak. To be spiritually mature, we must become as children. To have eternal life we must die to ourselves. Why then do we continue to misunderstand the message of power though submission? Jesus himself gave us the primary example when he submitted to his Father, even unto death. Yet, after accepting all the paradoxes in Christian doctrine, we reject the simple one of submission.

I like to refer to submission as spiritual buoyancy. Faith is like floating. In order to float, you must yield your entire body to the water. You must release control and preconceived notions that might hinder surrender, or you will drown. We are all commanded to submit; to let go and let God. Men, women, children, angels, the earth and Jesus—all must submit to the oracles of God. Not to lose yourself to a man, but to find yourself in Jesus. If we embrace the power of being a woman and stop regarding it as confinement, we can reclaim our children and change the world around us.

Through the power of Christian drama, we can examine unexplored territory. We can stimulate candid communication and expose hidden issues. Drama workshops can promote reflection within women and lead some to paths of recovery. They can provide opportunities for a healthy release of bottled-up emotions and assist the Spirit of God in healing pains of the past. Imagine the impression on the communities we work in if we could use our gifts to reach beyond our comfort zones. We can impact the life of someone who is seeking the motivation for change.

How will we ever know what God has empowered us to do if we do not trust him enough to try? Begin by totally submitting yourself to him. Become God's instrument of praise, his temple of worship. God knows your song. Let him play you. When you submit as an instrument in his hands, he will evoke the sweet song of service from the gift he has placed within you.

Geannetta Bennett is married to Donald Bennett, minister of the Northside Church of Christ in Hartford, Connecticut. They have three children, Anthony, Victoria and Morgan. Geannetta serves as church secretary, Sunday school teacher, choral director and facilitator for several committees.

A graduate of the Academy of Visual and Performing Arts and of Michigan Christian College with a degree in communication and theater, she has spoken and performed for various educational, civic and Christian functions throughout the country.

Owner and director of Principle Performance, a theater production company, she wrote and directed "My Soul Sings," a gospel *a cappella* musical, and is currently completing several other productions.

10

'He Leadeth Me'

D'Esta Love

March 1992

It is a familiar setting. It is the church that has nurtured me from my birth, and its beliefs, as well as its rhythms and practices, are ingrained in my being and speak to who I am in my truest self. It is a setting pregnant with memory. It is the church at worship. It echoes the rich tones of a cappella singing, the sound of my own voice blended with those of the congregation. If I listen, I can almost hear the sermons of my husband, my father before him, and now my son. This is a place that breathes comfort and blessing. This is where I belong. My roots go deep into the soil of my religious heritage. I am at home here. This is my family.

It is a Sunday evening service with its characteristic informality and ease. On this particular evening the church has gathered to pray. Our minister has set the tone for the evening with a litany of individual and communal needs and concerns, blessings and praise, and he has invited the congregation to join him in prayer. The invitation is clear and unmistakable, "Anyone who wants to may pray." Often before in times of worship and spontaneous prayer, I excluded myself because I knew that "anyone" did not mean me. However, this time I am certain I have been invited to pray.

As I sit beside my husband, I feel a growing eagerness and desire to give voice to the words welling up—for a lifetime—within me. But this is not the privacy of someone's home or a gathering of women for a Bible class or a special lecture series. This is the sanctuary of the church gathered at prayer, and I have been invited to participate in what, until now, has been forbidden in my religious experience. Can I, after 52 years, break the silence? I listen silently and with pounding heart as one by one, with complete freedom and spontaneity, men stand in all corners of the auditorium to pray. I marvel at the ease with which they pray. Their words flow with a familiarity unknown to me, and I sit frozen. It is intimidating. After a lifetime of silence in the sanctuary of God, I cannot utter a word.

Suddenly and unexpectedly I am caught in a deep, internal struggle. I have been given permission, and I want to pray, but I cannot. The tears that accompany the tightening in my throat are of hurt, anger, shame and fear. This is my church home; yet, for the first time in my life, I feel fear in the house of God. I am surrounded by people who love me, and I am comfortable here. The minister has extended an invitation to me to pray, so why am I silent?

I am silent because I respect my religious tradition, and it is precious to me. I am silent because I do not want to shatter the calm or disturb the peace I feel in this place. There are those present who will be offended if I pray—who will consider my prayer a violation of a direct command from the Word of God. The "forbidden" words I am about to utter could leave turmoil in their wake. I love this church and all it represents to others and to me, and I do not want to bring it harm.

I am not only silent, I am also afraid. I am afraid because of memories that rush into my mind. I remember how I felt 30 years earlier when the elders removed Randy from my Sunday school class. He was ten years old and had been baptized the previous week. Randy was a baptized male believer, and it was considered unsuitable for me, a woman, to continue teaching him the stories of Jesus. I also remember, several years later, when the elders of another congregation asked Stuart and me to teach a Wednesday night class in the church auditorium. At the conclusion of our lesson an individual expressed his disapproval and declared that we had set a dangerous precedent. To conclude his remarks, he read 1 Peter 3:1-6. As I sat on the front pew before the congregation, the words exhorting a woman to adorn herself in "a gentle and quiet spirit" made me feel exposed and shameful, and they ring in my ears even now as I contemplate accepting this invitation to pray.

I hesitate to pray because I do not want an impulsive act on my part to hinder any progress that has been made concerning women and the utilization of their gifts in the Kingdom. Yet, this is not impulsive. I have been invited to pray.

So why am I afraid? I am afraid of hearing the sound of my solitary voice in this place of worship and among the congregation of the Lord. Although I hear the words of my prayer over and over in my silent self, I cannot speak them. After 52 years of silence, have I grown mute? Are there no words I can utter "to ascribe thee glory and honor"? Is it too late for me to bring my gift to the altar? "What language shall I borrow to thank thee, dearest friend, for this thy dying sorrow, thy pity without end?"

September 1992
It is another familiar setting, but less nurturing and comforting than the security and peace of the church at worship. It is Firestone Fieldhouse, the gymnasium on the campus of Pepperdine University. The occasion is our weekly convocation, and I have been asked by the president of the university to open the 1992-93 academic year with a prayer. As the dean of students, I have stood before this audience week after week for four years. I have presided over the program, introduced guest speakers and even shared my faith. Today, I have been asked to pray. It is a simple thing, but I once again I am afraid. I have known of this assignment for weeks. It has been a weighty decision for the university, one that was made after two years of prayerful and diligent study. Although I had no part in making the decision, I participated in many of the discussions, and I am well aware of the sensitivity involved, as well as the possible ramifications. It has been a courageous decision for the university to make, and I

anticipate it will be controversial. Until now, women have not been allowed to lead prayer or to read scripture in our convocation programs. Today we are empowering our women to participate fully in the spiritual life of the university.

I am empowered by the significance of the moment, but I am apprehensive about the exposure—not just for the university, but for me. My name will be attached to this prayer, and word of my participation will spread. As the daughter of a preacher, I know too well the concern about what others will think. My motives will be critiqued by people who do not know me, in places I have never been. I will be labeled and judged by individuals who do not know my heart. And I am fearful of censure from those who know and love me.

Somehow I feel that God has called me to this task. He has placed me in this place at this moment. So why am I afraid? I am 52 years old, and yet I fear the disapproval of my parents. My father always encouraged my mother and his daughters to pray at home. He invited women to pray (a bold move in his day) in the numerous ladies' Bible classes he taught. But I do not know what my parents will think about this decision and my part in it. On the other hand, I am concerned that this public prayer will bring criticism to my parents and their ministry, as well as to our son and his work in the Kingdom.

Due to the public nature of this prayer, I am once again haunted by memories of other public experiences in which I faced disapproval. On one such occasion, Stuart and I conducted a weekend seminar for a congregation and taught side by side in the "private" space of the fellowship hall. We were also asked to teach a combined adult Bible class on Sunday morning, conducted in the "public" space of the auditorium. Stuart introduced our lesson, while I stood at his side. The moment I began to speak, part of the audience rose and walked out. I vividly remember how the minister, after the class was over, wept unabashedly as he apologized. I also remember when we were introduced to a Wednesday night audience in the auditorium of another congregation. At the last minute, it occurred to the individual presenting us to "put it to a vote" as to whether I should be allowed to teach with Stuart. His question was, Does anyone have a problem with D'Esta teaching us tonight? One person objected, so I was asked to remain seated while Stuart taught the class. These were uncomfortable moments, and I feel that discomfort today.

I feel the weight of the past and the responsibility placed in my hands as I await the beginning of convocation. I express my fears to Stuart, who stands beside me. His words ring clearer and truer than any others, "Do not be afraid. Forget about what others will think or say. When you step to the podium, just enter your closet and pray." I feel that God is calling me to courage. "Prince of Peace control my will; bid this struggling heart be still. Bid my fears and doubtings cease; hush my spirit into peace."

March 1996

I did step into my closet when I led that prayer in the fall of 1992, and it was a singular moment in my spiritual pilgrimage. I experienced God's faithfulness, and I believe he led me to that moment. A deep and abiding calm came over me, and I felt anointed by God's spirit. Since then, I have led other prayers in convocation. There have been other invitations to pray at Sunday evening services, and I have found the courage to respond. I am becoming less fearful in response to the call of God. I am discovering that most of my fears are unfounded, although a few are very real. News of my first prayer in convocation did appear in numerous church bulletins and journals. One headline read, "A Late Item on D'Esta Love of Pepperdine University." It informed the congregation that "There are indeed wolves among us" and concluded with a final pronouncement, "Depart from me, I never knew you." I received letters from people I did not know telling me I should "hang my head in shame."

However, I received far more letters and calls expressing encouragement. One letter included a poem that ended with the words:

The ancient way more clearly seen
    may open doors some day.
God grant that I before I die
    shall hear my daughter pray.

I also found occasion to talk with my parents about my fears and my views concerning greater opportunities for women to use their gifts in the Kingdom. To my surprise, I found them encouraging and supportive. I regret that I let fear keep me from discussing these matters with them earlier. Their love and support have given me courage, and we have been liberated from fear as together we explored, with openness and trust, the unspoken concerns of our hearts. The captives have been set free, for it is our fear that enslaves us. But God is faithful when we seek his will and make ourselves known to him and others.

January 2000

This entry returns me to the Malibu Church of Christ on a Sunday morning. I am not surprised today as Lucy stands before the congregation to read the Word of God in our hearing, and Kim, Megan, Alan and Tim lead us in singing. Nor am I surprised when Charlie and Martha, Tom and Beth serve communion. There is a sense of ease and comfort as men and women together serve this meal that testifies to one body in Christ. I am touched at the dedication of a newborn baby by the precious reading of scripture by Sarah Young and Sam Perrin, young children in our congregation, and I no longer have to wonder who will tell Sarah when she is a woman that she can no longer read the Word of God in the presence of his people. No one gets up to leave, and there is no public statement of disapproval from the audience. Rather, there is harmony and wholeness in the ways in which our various gifts are being used and our voices are being heard.

How can this be? It can be because on May 17, 1998, the elders of the Malibu Church of Christ made a statement to the church that made it possible for women to read from the Scriptures, to serve communion to the congregation, and to participate in periods of prayer in our worship. The reading of this statement was another significant moment in my life. We had all come to the morning service with great expectation, knowing that an announcement was going to be made, but not knowing what it would be. We listened with intensity and with tears as the elders addressed the needs of this particular congregation.

The statement read by John Wilson on behalf of the elders recounted the years of Bible study and prayerful attention given to the decision. The elders acknowledged the influence of women in the congregation. This was possible because several months before the decision was made, the elders invited a significant number of women in the church to meet with them in groups of six or seven. I was one of those women. I remember telling them that after being a preacher's daughter for over 50 years, as well as a preacher's wife, this was the first time a group of elders had invited me to tell them who I am. It was an emotional meeting for me. Through tears, I spoke of my personal journey of faith and the ways in which I felt my own religious tradition, for which I have great love, had let me down. I also spoke of a sense that time was running out for me, that in my lifetime I would not be able to hear a woman's voice speak in our sacred assembly, except to make an announcement regarding the children's ministry or a women's retreat. I spoke of my calling to ministry and of being gifted by God with words and a ministry of the Word. My question to them was, "What does the church do with a woman like me?" They listened as I and six other women spoke that night. They received the words of our hearts, which did not return to us void.

There were tears on that Sunday morning as well. They came from joy, with a full realization of what this decision meant for these elders and the church. I knew the courage it required as each elder spoke and prayed on behalf of the church. One elder confessed the sin of neglect and asked for forgiveness. I whispered to myself, "all these years," and I cried for all the years of silence. But my heart embraced their good news, and I embraced these courageous and humble men of God.

With joy I have brought my gifts to the altar. I have served communion, read scripture, and participated in open seasons of prayer. God has gifted me with the language of the Word, and I am blessed when I can read scripture. It is also a blessing of grace to serve communion to my brothers and sisters in Christ. Although I still find it uncomfortable to pray aloud in the assembly, it humbles me to lend my voice to the petitions and praise that rise up before our God.

I now confess that my faith was small and my expectations were based on the past and not on the workings of God in the hearts of sensitive men and women concerned with issues of justice and mercy and who have the courage to step out into uncharted waters as they seek to do God's will for this church. That morning we all confessed our sins. We prayed for God's power in the life of the church and for wisdom to pursue this bold new course.

God has blessed this church for its courage. The church was not split, and there is a new spirit of fellowship among us. We are growing in numbers and in our trust in God to be faithful. We have not fully arrived; there is more to do. But the voices of women are being heard in our assembly, and their gifts are being recognized.

Reflection

Today, as I look beyond the Malibu Church of Christ and my particular experiences as a woman growing up in this religious tradition, I see great changes taking place. The days when Randy was removed from my Sunday school class are almost gone. Rarely are Stuart and I censured for teaching scripture together in any setting. Greater avenues of service are opening for women in the church, and we are doing a better job of helping both men and women identify their gifts. We have more women in graduate Bible programs in our Christian colleges and universities, preparing to give their lives to the service of the Lord, and I am confident he will find ways to use them. We live in a time of struggle and change, but a time for courage and hope.

I am encouraged by the prayers of other women and am discovering that I am not alone in my journey. I have found both men and women faithfully searching God's word to discover his will as we face the challenging issues of Christian ministry for women. We are finding tools for the analysis of scripture which allow us to view the role of women in the larger context of the biblical witness, rather than allow two heavily disputed passages to relegate women to a silent role.

Recently I sat in on a graduate course at Pepperdine that Stuart taught on "Women in the Early Church and Today." One evening a young woman in the class presented her research on Romans 16. As she concluded her presentation, in which she discussed the implications of Paul's references to Phoebe, Priscilla, Mary, Junia, Julia and other women who had labored with Paul in his ministry, she asked the class (and the church), "Why have I not heard of these women before now? Why have I never heard a sermon on Romans 16?"

Only a few weeks ago Ken Durham, minister for the Malibu Church of Christ, preached a sermon on Romans 16. As I left the auditorium I heard several people echo the questions of the young woman in Stuart's class. "This is the first time I heard a sermon that recognized the work of Phoebe and the other women Paul commends." "I never knew there were so many women mentioned in Romans 16." We continue to make progress in our careful study of scripture and are finding that women of faith had significant roles in the ministry of the early church.

As I reflect on my journey, I see the hand of God working in my life to shape my ministry. I believe he called me into the life of Stuart Love, to be his partner and to walk by his side where God would lead us. I believe he called us to Pepperdine University and has opened doors of opportunity for service that could not have been possible elsewhere. I believe he called me to be dean of students, where I have had a rich and meaningful ministry among the students of Seaver College. And I believe he called me to lead that opening prayer in convocation, as I believe he has been at work in the life of the Malibu Church of Christ, bringing change and opening doors through which we can move into expanded areas of service in his name. This is the work of God, in his own good timing. And he is faithful as we prepare to serve him better and wait upon him in faith.

As I continue to give myself to God's leading of my life, I find that I am becoming more courageous in my faith. I do not mean to imply that I am "charging the gates"; I am not. But I am less content to hide behind my "walls of silence." I feel an obligation to others who are making this journey, and I am empowered to make myself known. I am also more secure in my understanding of scripture that calls me to witness to my faith, to lend my voice in praise to my king, to "lift up holy hands," and to speak his name in prayer.

131

I conclude with one last entry. I write this on June 1, 2001. Last month, Andrew Benton, president of Pepperdine University, appointed me to a new position. Beginning in the fall semester, 2002, I will begin my duties as university chaplain. Once again I wonder at the work of God and at his timing. During this coming academic year I will complete my Master of Divinity, and God is calling me to a new ministry. I am 60 years old, and God has been faithful. He has led me through years of preparation, and now, as I move into my last years at Pepperdine he has placed me in a position that fulfills all that I am and toward which my life has been moving.

As I look back on my life, I return to a scene in Fort Worth, Texas. I see a young girl sitting on the floor listening to her daddy preach on the radio. No other member of my family remembers the theme song of that radio program, but I do. The song was, "He Leadeth Me," and somehow I knew at the age of 12 that God was calling me. Whenever I hear it, I am taken back to that scene where I first heard the call of God. And I realize that he has been faithful. He has opened doors in his own good timing and he has led me into paths of service in his name. I don't know what this new ministry will be or what it will mean for my life, but this I know, "'Tis God's hand that leadeth me."

D'Esta Love is university chaplain at Pepperdine University, where she also serves as adjunct professor of religion. She holds an M.A. in English from Abilene Christian University and is a candidate for the M.Div. at Pepperdine.

D'Esta is a frequent speaker at retreats and lectureships and, with her husband Stuart, conducts worshops on marriage, leadership and biblical studies. Together with their son Mark, the Loves have authored a book entitled *Good News for Marriage*. They are also co-editors of *Leaven*, a journal for ministry in the Restoration heritage.

D'Esta and Stuart have been married for 42 years. They have two sons and four grandsons.

11

Trust Grows Up

Philis Boultinghouse

I vividly remember sitting between my mom and dad on an unpadded pew in a small East Texas church. Holding a blue *Songs of the Church* songbook, I would sing along with my parents, who made sure our whole family was at every single church service—even every night of the annual two-week-long gospel meeting. My mother's beautiful soprano had a touch of vibrato that made her jaw pulsate just a bit on the long notes. And my father would drop his chin slightly toward his chest (that posture seemed to help him hit the low notes), hold his songbook high, and with a serious look of concentration confidently and wholeheartedly belt out every word of every song.

If there were problems or tensions in that little church—and surely there were—I never knew it. Sitting between my parents on that hard pew, I felt completely safe and secure. I trusted my parents, and I trusted their God.

A Journey of Faith

As I grew into a young woman, I began to develop a faith of my own. After years of watching my mother sit at her small bedroom desk studying her Bible, I began to study my Bible in my own room. I was so proud the day my father brought home a varnished hardwood door—

complete with a doorknob hole—that he set up on cinder blocks as a desk in my room. I was the only one on the block with a door-desk—maybe the only one in town—and I loved it. My first serious study was of 1 Corinthians. I was thirteen years old, and I outlined the whole book.

My young faith grew in a gentle, loving environment; and I began to learn about trusting God. But my untested faith was simplistic and naive. I trusted God to keep my life free from disappointment and pain. I trusted him to bring me a perfect husband and make me a perfect wife. I trusted that my children would be obedient and sweet because of my perfect teaching, discipline and love.

I trusted that my relationships with my spouse, my children, my parents, my in-laws, my siblings, my church family and my coworkers would always be close, loving … easy. I trusted him to use me in his Kingdom and that his work for me would always be invigorating, rewarding, fulfilling and successful. I trusted that, if ever there were any problems in my Kingdom work or relationships, with a little bit of prayer and a sweet heart (which, of course, I would maintain at all times), all would be happily and quickly resolved.

I never once thought about trusting him in pain. I didn't imagine that I would need to trust him to guide me through dark times. I didn't know that to be instilled with the character of God I must be forged in the refining fire of pain. I didn't expect that I would have to be wronged before I could learn to forgive. I hadn't considered the possibility that the best way to learn patience is to be forced to wait. I had no idea that compassion grows out of despair or that peace is nurtured in the face of panic.

But then, trust grew up in me. It grew as I passed through dark times. It matured as things didn't turn out as I'd prayed. It deepened when I felt overcome with despair and failure. It took root and learned to hold on tight when the pain came.

The details of my pathway to a more mature faith will be different from yours, but the process is the same. Disappointment—no matter the source—shakes us all. Fear—whether related to our children's souls, adjusting to life without a spouse, or swallowing the panic of cancer—has a way of eating away at our facades of composure and perfection. And pain—no matter the source—always hurts. It is through this refining fire that trust grows up in us all.

Of course, this trusting woman has many years of learning ahead of her. Trust is far from grown in me. But my trust in the Lord is maturing as he peels layer after layer of pride from my heart, as he repeatedly encourages me to replace fear with faith, and as he wrestles with my heart, trying to teach me to put the interests of others above my own.

An Unexpected Career

My career in Christian journalism has really been just a framework for his maturing process. He could have done the same work in me in any number of life paths. But what a blessing it's been to grow up in this profession. What an honor to have worked with some of our fellow-ship's greatest leaders. I've had the privilege of working with and editing influential authors like Joe Beam, Rubel Shelly, Paul Faulkner, Lynn Anderson, Jeff Walling, Mike Cope, Terry Rush, Ron and Lyn Rose, Marvin Phillips, and more. From each I've learned something about what it means to be a child of God and to serve him in his Kingdom.

My introduction to the field that is now a sixteen-year career had nothing to do with my scholastic training or personal dreams, but it had everything to do with God's will alive in my life.

After experiencing a very sad and destructive church split, my husband and I and our two children, then five and eight, moved to West Monroe, Louisiana, where my husband, Denny, had grown up. We needed a temporary rest stop until we figured out what God had in store for our lives.

The church split had tested everything in me. It had shaken my view of how God works, for he certainly hadn't taken charge of the situation as I'd expected. And it had tested my love for his people. There's nothing like an emotionally-charged church conflict to bring out the very best and the very worst in brothers and sisters we think we know. I didn't know it then, but God was growing trust in my heart.

In West Monroe, Denny took a temporary job in the shipping department of a local business. I contributed to our income by cleaning houses. It was while I was folding laundry at our friend John Howard's house that Denny came bursting in the front door on a cool October morning in 1984.

"I have an idea!" he said breathlessly. "I want to start a new brotherhood publication—a magazine!"

Just a few months earlier, the *Firm Foundation*, a publication edited by the beloved and respected Reuel Lemmons, had been sold to men whose vision for the Lord's church was in sharp contrast to Mr. Lemmons's. He had no choice but to vacate the editorship. He would not be able to conform to the ideology of the new owners. Many in the Churches of Christ mourned the loss grievously. Under Lemmons's leadership, the journal had been a vehicle for the exchange of thoughts, for honest examination of Scripture, and for discussion on the practices of men versus the central appeal of the New Testament church: Christ and his cross. Under the new management, the paper took an entirely different approach, and that left mainline Churches of Christ without a voice and forum for discussion.

"I want to begin a contemporary magazine for the thoughtful, progressive Christian," he continued.

Immediately, we both knew that this was straight from the Lord. We were instantly filled with the fire of the dream. When we'd awakened that morning, we hadn't a clue as to what God had in store for us. Now we knew without a doubt.

Denny took his idea to John Howard, who quickly caught the vision. John, educated in business, put his pencil to paper, and the two of them came up with a plan to present to John's father—Alton Howard—a man whose absolute devotion to God and Christ's body on earth ranks him alongside Reuel Lemmons as one of the most influential men of his generation in the Churches of Christ. The big-hearted, generous Mr. Howard said, "Okay, boys, we'll give it a try!"

Denny, John and Alton all concurred that Reuel Lemmons needed to be part of this new venture. So Denny drove to Austin, Texas, to meet with this veteran of the faith. After patiently listening to Denny lay out his dream for the new publication, Reuel responded in his dry, Southern drawl: "I don't need to take on another work. My fishin' pole has been gathering dust in my closet for way too long." But he believed in the project and recognized that his involvement would open many doors that would otherwise remain closed. So this respected man of wisdom and experience agreed to work with this young whippersnapper. But, mind you, his role would be minimal. He still wanted some fishing time.

After several months of traveling across the country, getting input from leading men in the Churches of Christ, and gathering an impressive group of staff and contributing writers, Denny was ready to set up office. It was then that I began to think that I might prefer secretarial work to cleaning houses, and I proposed to Denny that I work for him.

Now, we knew that not every husband-and-wife team is cut out to work together, and since we didn't know whether we were one of the couples who was, we made a deal: I would begin work February 14, 1985. On May 1, we would reevaluate. If I didn't like working with Denny, I could step out of that position and there would be no questions asked, no feelings hurt. And if he didn't feel comfortable working with me, I would step out of that position and there would be no questions asked, no feelings hurt.

May 1 rolled around, and when we reviewed the previous two and a half months together, we both affirmed that we liked working together. We were a team! We had a small office, two telephones, two used desks, and some three-by-five file cards and a file box in which to maintain our subscription list.

The editorial arrangement was a simple one. The selected staff of writers, as well as many others, began sending a stream of articles for the new magazine. Denny, serving as managing editor, sent copies of articles to Mr. Lemmons. Reuel would select the articles as he saw fit, but always graciously allowed his young partner much input in the selection.

It was then that my editing "career" had its beginning. The writers were doing a great job of providing food for thought for the magazine, Reuel and Denny's article selection provided balanced, challenging reading for our new subscribers, and Denny handled all the communication, article solicitation, and day-to-day functions of the magazine.

Only one thing was missing. No one was in place to edit the articles for basic punctuation, grammar or logic flow.

My work load was very light back in those days—I answered the phone, kept up with the subscription list, and did a little typing for Denny—so I had plenty of time to study books on the basics of editing. And I wasn't shy about asking questions, so I began seeking out English teachers and others in our fellowship who could offer me assistance in my self-appointed role of copy editor. I took a few classes at the local university and soon discovered that I really liked this work.

At the time, I didn't fully comprehend what an honor it was to work with Alton Howard and Reuel Lemmons. But as the years have passed, my appreciation for them and gratefulness for my interaction with them has grown.

Then in 1987, Howard Publishing—which at that time published mostly hymnals and only a few books, written by folks in our fellowship—moved into one of Alton's recently vacated buildings. There was plenty of room for Denny and me and our new subscription manager, so *IMAGE* and Howard Publishing became roommates.

One afternoon as I was reading one of Howard Publishing's few books, I noticed several errors. The book was about to be reprinted, so I asked Alton if I could do some light editing on the book before it went back to press. He agreed to my proposal. The first book I edited was *Churches of Christ* by Ed Wharton.

Howard Publishing and my role in it have changed dramatically since those early days. For several years, I split my time between Howard Publishing and *IMAGE*. Then, in 1994, when *IMAGE* magazine was sold to *Wineskins*, Denny and I both became full-time employees of Howard Publishing. The Lord had prepared the way for *IMAGE*, and he then prepared the way for both of us to enter the broader publishing world of Howard Publishing.

As I write this in July 2001, I serve as managing editor for Howard Publishing and director of our "EPD Team"—the Editorial, Production and Design Team. This department currently has seven full-time, in-house employees and several part-time, off-site freelance workers. Our department takes a "raw" manuscript to printed book.

I know that for many women—whether in or out of the church setting—their gender proves to be an unfair hindrance to their careers. I've not known this with the Howards. Besides being a publisher, Alton Howard is also an author, and I've had the privilege of editing many of his writings. When I began working with him, I'd not had much editing experience, I was much younger than he, and to top it off, I was a woman. For many of his generation, that combination evoked disrespect and dismissal. Yet, from the first time I worked with him, Alton has treated me with respect and has even allowed this now not-so-young woman to argue with him over words he wrote and ideas he expressed. I've never ceased to be in awe of that attitude. And it's an attitude that he passed down to his son, John Howard, who now serves as president of Howard Publishing.

The opportunities afforded to me through Howard Publishing brim with blessings from God. Not only is the work rewarding and exciting, but it is in this workplace that I have experienced "up close and personal" what it means for men and women to work together for the cause of God's Kingdom.

My Rights versus What's Right for the Church
In sorting out the role of women in the church, we must first wrestle with the tension between my rights and what's right for God's family on earth. Our first concern must not be achieving our personal agendas but using the gifts God has given us for the advancement of his Kingdom. We must continually ask ourselves how his sanctified Body can best represent Christ to the world, how it can mature its own members, and how it can create the kind of church that draws others to Christ. In answering these questions, both women and men will find guidelines for their roles in today's church.

The beginning place must be in laying ourselves aside. And that's so hard! Did God really mean it when he told us through the apostle Paul to "consider others better than [ourselves]"? Does he really expect us to "look not only to [our] own interests, but also to the interests of others"? (Phil. 2:3-4). I think he does.

When we asked Christ to become Lord of our lives, we relinquished our rights as individuals. When we put on Christ in baptism, he became our identity, and he alone. When we allowed Christ to come into ourselves, he displaced the self that reigned upon our hearts' thrones.

As the Lord has worked in me over the past several years, he has repeatedly reminded me to press out of my heart the sin of pride and self-centeredness. Pride is a sin that demands to be fed with recognition, appreciation and respect.

You know the feeling: Someone questions your decision at work or doesn't invite you to serve in a leadership role at church. Maybe your talents are overlooked or your long hours of work are unappreciated. You feel that rising indignation—"righteous indignation" we sometimes call it. But there's nothing righteous about it. Its father is the father of lies. He lies to us and tells us we must demand appreciation and respect. That's the feeling we must train our hearts to recognize and teach ourselves to supplant.

The effort to purge our hearts of pride is a daily battle—at least it is for me. Pleasing ourselves instead of God is a humanity-wide problem. It began with Adam and Eve in the Garden, and it continues with each of us. But the more we learn to lay ourselves and our personal agendas aside, the more we become precious and valuable tools in his hand. The less we pursue recognition and advancement for ourselves, the more God can work through and in our lives. But the purging process is never pleasant.

Unfortunately, there's no better cure for pride than to be slapped in the face with failure. There's no better remedy for a judgmental attitude than to come face to face with our own frailties. Nothing can cure us of self-righteousness more quickly than having our weaknesses revealed by the light of his truth.

Years of sinning and being made aware of my failures have served me well. For as I see myself for who I truly am—a sinner, redeemed only by the blood of Christ—I become a little bit more like the one who gave his all for me and a little less concerned about my rights in his church.

Discerning the Issues

As we become the trusting women God has called us to be by laying ourselves aside and thinking first of the needs of others, including the needs of our church families, we are ready to ask the next questions: What church practices and ideologies need to be challenged because they harm the witness of Christ? What restrictions are we placing on God-given gifts that he intends to serve his Body?

The Bible is clear. God has given each of us gifts that he expects us to use to edify and encourage his Body: "Each one should use whatever gift he has received to serve others, faithfully administering God's grace in its various forms" (1 Pet. 4:10). What if the church member with the most financial savvy and experience is a female bank president? Will the church ignore her gifts because she is a woman? Such an approach could be detrimental to crucial decisions. What if the uncontested behind-the-scenes leader in a mission effort is a woman? Will she be denied the public leadership role that can best advance her vital ministry?

"Now to each one the manifestation of the Spirit is given for the common good" (1 Cor. 12:7). Has the Spirit manifested himself in women only through the gifts of preparing communion, washing baptismal clothes, and cooking for potlucks? Obviously not! All we have to do is ask women what they do in the professional world or observe their leadership gifts as they work in women's ministries or notice the organizational and multi-tasking skills required for the young stay-at-home mom.

Do we really reflect the integrity of Christ when a female children's minister is given less authority in her realm than the male youth minister is given in his? Does the church authentically reflect Christ when women are treated with disrespect and their input not sought out and valued? Do we lift up our Lord and draw others to him when we rigidly hold to human traditions and a fifties culture? The answers to questions like these will tell us which issues are worth taking a stand on. However, our decisions must be based on what is best for the maturing of Christ's Body on earth and its message to the lost souls around us.

But no matter what kind of church environment we find ourselves in—one that respects and uses women or one that overlooks and dismisses their gifts—who we are in Christ is not defined by what we are and are not "allowed" to do. It is not defined by what others write or say on the role of women in the church. We are defined by the God who created us, who daily shapes us, and to whom we belong.

Women of God are just as concerned about pleasing their Lord as are men. Women whose hearts are subject to the King of Kings can be trusted to live out the role of servant, alongside their male co-heirs, in God's Kingdom. As a united Body of men and women, we can raise our voices in the song I remember singing as a child, "None of Self and All of Thee."

Philis Boultinghouse serves as managing editor for Howard Publishing Company in West Monroe, Louisiana. She has recently become an author in her own right with the publication of two gift books, *Hugs for Sisters* and *Heavenly Mail, Words of Encouragement*.

Philis speaks for women's groups and participates in the teaching ministry of her local congregation.

She has been married for 30 years and is the mother of two grown children.

12

Sinking and Soaring

Joy McMillon

A wise friend once told me, "There are times in all our lives in which we soar, and there are times in which we sink."

"I am definitely in a sink hole," I thought as I drove the lonely 20 miles back home from my parents' house. I was feeling emotionally and spiritually drained. Too much was happening. Trying to meet the needs of aging, ailing parents. Managing a demanding schedule as editor of the *Christian Chronicle*. Our son, diagnosed with melanoma, though he seemed to be doing well after his surgery.

"Lots of people have done this," I told myself. I had known many other women who had gone through more stressful events than these. I guess I never realized what a toll it took on them. I remember asking myself that night, "How did I get to such a low point—emotionally and spiritually?"

My life had been almost embarrassingly happy. An only daughter, I was reared in a happy home where Christian faith was not only taught but modeled. I can't remember not believing in God, loving Jesus, or relishing Vacation Bible School. Life was good.

Thanks to conscientious Bible teachers such as Sister Schott and Brother Coiner, I had known the books of the Bible since second grade. From childhood on, I was familiar with the major stories of the

Bible and could recite my share of facts. Later, I graduated from a Christian university and married a wonderful man. We had been blessed with two precious sons.

But, somehow, when these stressful personal situations began to pile up, God and Jesus seemed far away. Later that night after I drove into our garage, I sat in the silent darkness, trying to sort out my feelings and thoughts.

Time pressures and family responsibilities demanded that I resign from my rewarding work with the *Chronicle*. I had already made plans to do that and had made my peace with the decision. It would be best for everyone. But something else was wrong, something even deeper was troubling me. What had become of my joy, my peace, the sense of closeness I had always felt with my Lord? "This is ironic," I thought. "Here I am, blessed with the privilege of writing and speaking about faith, and all I feel is dry and empty."

My journey of faith has taken me in a variety of directions with many opportunities to see the Lord at work in my life and ministry. Some of the roads have been exciting and fulfilling, but some have seemed more like an uphill trek. Of course any journey that didn't include potholes, dark stretches, dead ends and unexpected detours wouldn't require much faith, would it?

That night as the tears rolled down my face, one proverb flashed continually through my mind: "Trust the Lord with all your heart and lean not on your own understanding." That proverb has sat, framed, on my desk for years. But that was the problem. For years I had been living on a comfortable, safe plateau. Everything had gone well in my life. Now I found myself undergoing one of life's tests, and I was shocked and disappointed with the level of my faith. I discovered that I didn't have much practice in trusting the Lord when the chips were down. I didn't know how to rest in peace on his everlasting arms when the storms of life flooded over me.

I desperately needed help, and God and the Bible were the only places I knew to turn. In the next few months, when I felt empty and overwhelmed, when I didn't have any peace or answers, I would struggle in the early morning hours to grasp the depths of God's words. I sensed that I was drinking from a fountain that gave life to my soul. The words of John White resonated within me when I read his book, *The Fight*. About the effect of his own Bible study on his soul, he wrote:

> Foundations cemented themselves to an other-worldly rock beyond the reach of time and place, and I became more strong, and I felt more alive. I cannot express the wonder of finding that I, a neurotic, unstable, middle-aged man (woman, in my case) have my feet firmly planted in eternity. All of this came to me through a careful study of Scripture, for in the study I have experienced an ever deepening knowledge of a person, Jesus Christ, my Lord.

I could not express it in such an articulate way, but this was exactly how I felt! The Word became my salvation, my passion. I tried to read it as if I'd never picked up a Bible or entered a church building. I saw things I never realized were in scripture, or maybe these things had just never registered before. I saw things that didn't read at all as I had been taught. My sins were so much more painful to me now.

If I could talk for years about it, I don't think I could express what the study of God's word has come to mean to me. I am sure many of you have studied the word with greater intensity or in greater depth than I have. But the Bible has torn my life apart and remade it. And I am so grateful.

The more I studied, the more I wanted to study. So many interesting things to think about, so many questions to research. And that meant digging deeper. It was so exciting! It was as if God had lifted a veil that stood between him and me, and I began to experience him in a closer, more personal way. As the wise man said, I had tasted the Lord, and He was good! I began to hunger for an opportunity to encourage other women to drink deeply from this fountain and experience the same joy

Meanwhile, God in his gracious mercy was weaving people and circumstances together in such a way that my dream would soon become a reality. This is how it happened.

A few years later the staff of our local congregation asked me if I would consider beginning a women's ministry there. Mother had passed away, and my father, after suffering several debilitating strokes, was living in a nearby nursing home. Our two sons were healthy and grown. God's perfect timing.

I had always wanted to work with a women's ministry program. In fact, only four months earlier, a large church had tried to hire me and my husband to work on their staff. Many of their women had bolted from their Ladies' Bible Class in order to attend Bible Study Fellowship (BSF), a well-known, world-wide Bible study. Faced with a dwindling women's class, the elders wanted me to develop an in-depth Bible study that could challenge their women and bring them back home.

Lynn and I eventually declined their gracious offer, believing the Lord was leading us to stay where we were in Oklahoma City. But the dream of developing a Bible class that might attract women of all ages who were hungry for God's word captured my heart and mind. I began praying for the Lord to open an opportunity for me to do that. I didn't know how or when or even if this dream was part of God's plan for me, but I decided I would lay it before him and wait for an answer.

So when the church staff asked me to develop a women's ministry only four months later, I felt a little like Rhoda in Acts. Even though I had prayed for the door to open, it was almost too much to believe that the Lord was sending me a positive answer this quickly and in such a clear and powerful way.

I set to work researching as many women's ministries as I could find. The first part of the women's ministry I wanted to develop had to do with an in-depth Bible study. Our congregation had a wonderful Ladies' Bible Class, but some were asking what could be done to revitalize the class, build our enrollment, and attract younger women.

After much prayer and discussion, some of our women embarked upon a redesign of our weekday women's Bible study. Many people were part of the creative process. We decided to imitate the 50-year-old BSF format: a two-hour study, including small group discussions and a 30-minute lesson; daily Bible readings with questions; and take-home notes. Why not target the community with this Bible class? Why not welcome every seeker, regardless of her faith tradition, to study the word with us?

How would the women of our church feel about changing the traditional Ladies' Bible Class format? Would they embrace the concept, or would they reject it? Despite the risk, we needed to share our vision with others and get their reaction. We wanted it to be God's program, and if he wanted it to go, we trusted that it would.

The first thing I did was test the reaction of our minister's wife. She enthusiastically endorsed the program and urged me to continue developing the idea. She quickly became a strong right arm and a wise adviser. Together, in March of 1990 we chose a core group of 20 women of various ages with whom to share the vision of this new program. It was to be called the Center for Women's Biblical Studies (CWBS).

Our women needed to believe in it, or it could not and should not go forward. We wanted no part of anything that might be divisive. We told them about our dreams—of writing our own curriculum for in-depth Bible studies; of evangelizing our friends; of inviting believers of various faith traditions to engage in a textual study of the Bible, God's word.

If they approved, "Ladies' Bible Class" would undergo major surgery. It would become a community Bible class with visitors. No more announcements about our congregation's activities. No more discussion of our sick. No more planning of bridal and baby showers. No more talking among ourselves about "in-house" matters.

The format would require sacrificing some wonderful, comfortable traditions, finding another way to communicate important congregational information, and focusing on intense Bible study. We would need to step outside of our comfortable friendships and be more concerned with welcoming into our building those strangers who might venture in.

I suspect our presentations to the women that day were passionate. All I know is that they listened carefully, and then they began to ask questions. Lots of them. Creative ideas began to spark like fireworks around the room as woman after woman got excited. It was like watching a prairie fire spread as the women volunteered to do anything we needed.

Our hearts were bursting with joy as we prayed and hugged each other at the meeting's conclusion. Once again, our Lord had delivered "more than we could ask or imagine." We praised God for all he had done and all he was going to do. We prayed that he would grant us the wise leaders we would need to make the plan a reality by fall.

Eventually, we presented our proposal to the elders, who enthusiastically supported our "make-over." Verbally and financially, they remain our greatest encouragers.

For the program to work, we knew we needed a spirit of shared responsibility. And we knew that would occur only when women participated in the decision making, carried out the functions of the ministry, shared their ideas, and helped implement the change. All of that was well underway in April.

In September, 1990, a redesigned CWBS opened its doors to our community. We had advertised on billboards and in the newspaper, and our first year, attendance increased by 28 percent. More important, several visitors from the community had entered the study.

This fall we begin our thirteenth year. Last fall, our enrollment was 227; almost 15 percent annually have been visitors. Some have put the Lord on in baptism; many more have grown closer to the Lord. God has lavishly blessed CWBS with wonderful, committed servant leaders through the years.

Today, we have developed eight years' of curriculum, questions and notes. At the end of those eight years, we start over, studying books from the Old and New Testament. God brought Jeanette Kee Schoof to the Memorial Road Church at just the right time. An excellent thinker and student of the Word, she prepared our daily questions. Every summer, as she worked on the Herculean task of writing curriculum for the next year, she laughingly threatened to move to Alaska. But, thank God, she never did,

I wrote the accompanying notes, compilations of Biblical scholarship and comments on each lesson. Each participant receives a copy of these notes as she is leaving. I also lead the teaching session following group discussion meetings. These two roles are labor-intensive, consuming 25 to 30 hours weekly.

Several groups have expressed an interest in our material, but, unfortunately, we haven't had time to properly edit and publish it. That continues to be part of the long-term plan.

Whether a church is beginning a new women's ministry, resurrecting a lifeless one, or enhancing a growing program, a major challenge will be developing and training leaders. By that I mean energizing and motivating women to open their eyes to their spiritual gifts, and helping them stretch and grow. Leadership development is an act of loving and leading key women. Tell them and show them that you love them, that you are dedicated to them, and that you want to help them use their gifts in God's service. You will grow close to these women as you plan, prepare and pray together. I always tell them they are "far above rubies," and they are.

Our leaders meet from 9:30 until 11:00 each Wednesday as we go over our lessons for the week, pray for our students, and prepare for class the next day.

A significant area of challenge has been child care. At first we started out, as BSF does, with a volunteer children's leader who recruited the volunteer teachers for our classes. We found this impossible to sustain, however, and our staff of 15 child care personnel and a coordinator are now paid by the church. With the beginning of Sonshine School, a Tuesday/Thursday school in our building, and a pool of nearby Oklahoma Christian University students, we are now able to provide good quality child care and effective Bible classes for the children much more smoothly.

Our program has proved popular, because it meets many of the spiritual needs of women. Often women quit work so they can be a part of CWBS. It is not perfect; we have made our share of mistakes. We have learned that publicity is very valuable to inform the community about the Bible class. We rent billboards, advertise in local newspapers, and publish brochures for women to hand to their friends. But we need to do more and smarter advertising.

I used to write from eight to ten pages of notes for each lesson, but we have learned most people won't read that much material. Now I write three to four. We have learned that recruiting leaders demands complete honesty about the time commitment involved. Leaders will be committing to two mornings a week; they must do their own lessons, of course; and they are expected to call each class member weekly.

We have seen the hard way that, when leaders do not follow through, their classes lose students. These women do not feel a personal connection and loyalty to their group. We have also learned that, although some are conscious of including visitors, it is difficult to keep others from talking with one another about "in-house" activities and ignoring visitors.

But we are learning to grow from our mistakes and celebrate our successes. They are really God's successes, not ours. Every year we receive notes from women who tell us what a blessing CWBS has been to them and to their families. Even some husbands have written to thank us for the changes the study has made in their wives and their marriages. Women value the love and shared community it has nurtured. It has opened their eyes to the excitement of living in a close, personal relationship with their Lord

Here are a few suggestions based on our experience:

First, I would urge every Christian woman to follow her passion in the Lord. When we are passionate about something—a song, a project, a ministry—then we can transcend our fear. The excitement of the goal overrules our self-doubts. Believing in your ministry eliminates stress and strain. Your relationship with the clock and the calendar changes. Frequently, I look at the clock and am stunned that three or four hours have passed so quickly.

Second, expect some rejection. Though we have had few negative comments, circumstances may vary. Remember the advice of Eleanor Roosevelt, and "learn to grow the hide of a rhinoceros." Be loving; be kind; go slowly if need be; and try not to take negative comments too personally. They usually mean someone is frightened and needs reassurance. Take the rebuffs graciously, and reroute the criticism. You can usually silence critics by anticipating them. Have an answer for each possibility.

Third, be persistent. Believe in your work, hang on and reconfigure. Avoid words that provoke people. Look at the person who may oppose you as someone who is holding a valuable truth. Avoid personal agendas. Dedicate yourself to the study of (and, of course, obedience to) the Word. Remember, people need to see Jesus in your life and attitudes.

A friend of mine wanted to establish a women's ministry. Her proposal was turned down with little or no explanation. She asked for a meeting with several of the elders. In a kind, non-threatening way she asked them, "What troubles you about this?" They spoke plainly, and she was able to answer the criticism and allay their fears. She was allowed to begin a women's ministry the next year.

Finally, don't be afraid. Understand who is on your side. The Lord God Almighty. Then, remember to "trust in the Lord with all your heart, and lean not upon your own understanding."

Joy McMillan is a teacher, speaker, editor and writer. She served as managing editor of the *Christian Chronicle* and has produced two audio cassette series, *Family Making* and *A Woman's World*.

A graduate of Oklahoma Christian University, she holds the MA degree from the University of Central Oklahoma. She teaches Bible at Oklahoma Christian and has spoken for women's days and lectureship throughout the US and in several foreign countries.

For the past 20 years she and her husband have presented the Family-making series and Effective Christian Parenting seminars. They have two sons and four granddaughters.

13

Faithfulness: His and Mine

Julie Magos

"He who began a good work in you . . ."
God created me, determining the times set for me and the exact places where I should live so I would seek him, reach out and find him. He is not far. He knows me, and he is faithful. I am the one who has struggled to locate the "place" he has determined for me to live. I love my birth family. My parents, Glenn and Janice Kramar, have loved God with all their heart, soul, mind and strength. Dad was from California, Mom from Iowa, and they were ministering to a congregation in New Jersey when I was born. We are eight siblings, six girls and then two boys. I am the fifth daughter.

I have few memories of the time in New Jersey. The house was big and white. We had church in the living room. Mostly, I remember trips and people. We traveled from coast to coast, visiting family and friends along the way. I don't remember ever staying in a motel or eating at a restaurant; we always had precious loved ones to commune with. They became images of my first years of life—names, faces and a sense of belonging to something much larger than just my family. Most often, they were "Church of Christ" people, my religious heritage.

Somewhere along the way, I began to form my concept of "me." Who was I? I remember liking to be among people, liking the feeling of belonging, also being on the shy side.

Our family enjoyed singing. The four-part harmony of my dad and his brothers' quartet still resonates deep inside me. We would sing at our morning devotions, sing in the station wagon driving across country. Mom would sing as she washed dishes and clothes. We learned a few songs to share in public: "White Coral Bells" and "There Was a Desperado" are two I remember. My four older sisters learned them better than I did. I remember on one occasion when my sisters were in line ready to sing at a friend's house, I hid behind the curtains, hoping not to be seen. Performing in public was uncomfortable for me.

When I was five years old, we moved to Lima, Peru, where my parents were to live and teach the Word for the next eight years of my life. I am overwhelmed with thankfulness to God for those years of being formed by my experiences and the lives of those around me. Mom and Dad were faithful in their teaching and living. I don't remember incongruity between what I heard and saw in them. Church was in our living room for the first three years. Mom made the communion bread in our kitchen, and the baptistry was in the backyard, doubling as a swimming tank in hot weather. The "church people" were my extended family. We ate, sang, prayed, traveled and shared life together. They were "we" to me. Our language was "Castellano," Spanish. My blood relatives were precious, but far away in those years.

It was with this blend of family, language and culture that I moved back to the United States in 1971. I was 14 years old and feeling very lost. I didn't understand the grief I felt and didn't have words to express it. So many experiences in life have a logical explanation but are oceans of confusion inside us.

We moved to my dad's birthplace, El Centro, California—the Imperial Valley desert where my grandparents were brave pioneers in the early 1900s. It was home to my dad but strange to me and terribly hot in August when we got there. At the high school, I sought out friends who spoke Spanish, but they called it "Español" and used different words I had to learn. The familiar was gone. Tortillas, tacos and beans took the place of pan francés, white rice and papa a la huancaína.

Mom and Dad found jobs teaching school, and Daddy preached on Sunday. We drove twenty miles to church and back twice on Sunday and again on Wednesday. There was a town closer to us with three Churches of Christ, but there had been some kind of division several years earlier, and they didn't "fellowship" each other. I didn't know that kind of thing existed. My grandmother commented that, when it all happened, people who used to call each other "brother" and "sister" would walk across the street not to have to greet each other.

Our church was small, about 60 people in a town of about 4,000. Church was in English. The people were friendly and happy for us to be "back." They had known us when we were babies. I had aunts, uncles and cousins there, which helped give me some sense of belonging, but mostly I just wanted to go back to my home in Lima, which didn't exist any more.

My belief in God was always present. We continued to have family devotions in the mornings. Life revolved around going to church, youth rallies and gospel meetings. We lived in the country on Grandma's farm with Mount Signal to the south, beautiful sunsets over the mountain range to the west and unending stars in the black skies at night. I would climb out onto the roof and lie on my back, staring at the stars and meditating on God, who placed them there—the God I knew was present, but who was not quite real to me yet.

I wanted to find God. I knew he was the answer. Somehow church didn't quite seem to make his presence known. Was he a God of rules—exactly how to sing, take the Lord's Supper, contribute money, exactly how long the hem of my dress should be? Did he know the lostness in my heart, and could he fill it? I wanted my friends to be Christians because I knew that was where the truth was, but I didn't know how to explain it, and sometimes church issues became embarrassing to me. Why didn't we go to the Church of Christ that was closer to our house? I couldn't explain it in a way that made sense—either to my friends or to me. Mostly, I just didn't invite them.

During the first month at the new high school, I was transferred into the advanced Spanish class. My seat was directly across from a friendly senior from Mexico, Manuel Magos. He was interested in me from the first day. I was a novelty to him—a "freckle-faced gringo from Peru who spoke perfect Spanish with hand expressions and all."

We became good friends in the midst of what was a strange country to both of us.

About two years later, I knew he was special to me, and I made the decision before God in prayer that somehow I would try to bring Manuel to know him. I invited Manuel to church that very night, and he came with us the next morning. It's an adventure to explain Church of Christ traditions to a Catholic. No crosses, images, kneeling, candles, robes. No musical instruments. You're supposed to read the Bible and prove that everything the preacher says is true. You know that this is the one true belief, but then you discover that the other church thinks they're the one true belief also. We have the same Bible, and both claim to come from the same beginning, Pentecost. What makes us each so right, or so wrong? This was the beginning of some real searching to define truth. I was confident that the Bible had the right answers, and that surely our church had the best understanding, but the explanations didn't always make sense.

Manuel was baptized at the end of the year. We went to Lubbock Christian College for a year and were married that summer, moving to Tucson to establish our new life. Manuel was consistent with his church attendance and involved in everything. He was thankful for his conversion to Christ and for the purpose in life and purity of heart Christ had brought him.

We decided to move back to the Imperial Valley where Manuel could work with his brother at the auto body shop, but Manuel wanted to spend some time in concentrated Bible study first. He didn't plan to be in full time ministry, but he wanted to be better prepared to teach classes and participate in the Kingdom wherever we lived. We sold our house in Tucson and moved to Lubbock for six months at Sunset Preaching School. Manuel studied in the Spanish program; I chose various classes and took care of our one-year-old son.

I had seen faith lived out in the lives of my parents in many ways through my growing-up years. I had seen love, mercy, grace, justice, sacrifice, tears, prayers and joy expressed. The few months at Sunset were a time for me to hear more of the structure of our heritage in Churches of Christ, learning the meaning of terms like hermeneutics, homiletics and Restoration Movement. I recall one lesson in chapel that emphasized that Jesus is Lord, and that nothing should be supreme over him, not even the Bible. The classes on Christian Evidences and Sacrificial Systems strengthened the foundations of my faith. Another class dealt briefly with women's role in ministry, taking the standard passages so literally as to teach that a woman should not even pray in the presence of her husband. I remember a sermon about worship being the way we live each day, not just coming to church. Those classes stimulated my thinking, but I didn't draw my own conclusions yet.

We moved back to the Imperial Valley, having gained new friendships and new knowledge and purpose for our lives. Manuel worked at the auto body shop, and I eventually finished my nursing degree at the local college. For the next seven years we were actively involved in the congregation where Manuel had been baptized. We organized youth rallies and taught classes. Manuel led singing and even preached in English.

We noticed a need for the Spanish-speaking people to hear the Word. One faithful sister came and sat every week with her Bible, though she didn't understand a word of English. Manuel and a newly converted couple, Barry and Denise Galindo, organized classes and preaching in Spanish, and soon a small, active group was meeting.

During these years, we learned what it was like in ministry—wanting to see greater faith and more conversions in so many lost lives, but frustrated by what seemed to be a system of rules and opinions that limited our efforts, and not knowing how to work through it. We were praying and fasting for God's will to be made known to us when we were called by the elders of the congregation in Escondido, California.

They had a vision of reaching out to Spanish-speaking people coming to California in search of work. The dream was to evangelize and grow a congregation where first-, second- and third-generation immigrants could worship together in spite of differing languages and customs. We dreamed of building "sister" congregations in towns along the border, and training and sending teams from the new converts all over Mexico. We were convinced that it was God's calling to us, and with much "fear and trembling" we moved to Escondido with our four young children in 1987.

"I always pray with joy because of your partnership in the gospel. . ."
The leadership of the church was united in their desire to live and preach the Word, to see souls converted to Christ and lives changed for eternity. The methods didn't matter so much, and different ones have been tried. I have learned much from the godly brothers and sisters in Escondido, and I am thankful to be here.

The first few years were times of hard work at home and in ministry. I was still evaluating many questions: What is a vocational ministry? Is there one "right" way to do it? What is a minister's wife? Is this a team job or two separate ministries? What is the essence of the gospel? What is salvation? How can I share something useful with a young mother who has just moved here from Mexico without legal documents and without an extended family, who doesn't understand anything about life here? What does it mean to be Christ-like, no matter what culture you're in?

I had determined to follow Christ no matter what it meant, but I wasn't sure how Christianity should be lived out in my life and in the lives of those I was teaching. There were more questions than answers.

The church leaders were struggling with issues of discipleship—"What does it mean to be a disciple?" They prayerfully decided to keep the congregation free of hierarchical methods of discipleship. I was relieved in my personal life, because my tendency to depend on others made it easier for me to be a follower than to struggle through faith issues on my own. I could obey rules to please others, but would I obey God with a clear conscience even if it went against people? I already realized that people of obedient faith through the centuries had come to differing conclusions about the same scriptures, and I wouldn't be satisfied just following one conclusion or another. I wanted to know who was right.

In addition to our four children (and two more who were born after we moved), we had a teenage "daughter" who lived with us and whom we adopted in our hearts. I wasn't working as a nurse any more, but spending many hours a week leading women's discipleship groups, visiting couples with my husband, and teaching one-on-one studies. I was burdened by the many needs of the families we were ministering to, as well as ministering to my own home and children. But I had answered some of my questions about how to share the essence of the gospel and the meaning of repentance, justification and sanctification. My faith had been renewed, and I felt joyful and purposeful.

"so you may be able to discern what is best . . ."

One of the questions that keeps coming back regards what is best. What is the pure gospel our Lord died for?

"Love God with all your heart, soul, mind and strength, and love your neighbor as yourself." This is what Jesus said is most important. This is what is best.

The exact details of what this means and how we can practice it in our daily lives is the work of faith of each of us, no matter where we live. This law can be lived in a wealthy suburban church or on the streets of a third-world country. This law applies whether you are in slavery or freedom. This is the law that has settled in my heart as the deciding factor in every situation.

The couples with whom we share the gospel are almost always from the religious tradition that was brought to this hemisphere by Spaniards in the sixteenth century. As I share with them the freedom from condemnation of sin, the liberation of grace, the emptiness of human traditions, I've often asked myself if I'm merely showing them another type of legalism. I have purposed not to do so. I don't want them to be bound again.

I know that as children we need laws and boundaries until we come to understand and assimilate the principles behind them. Galatians speaks of the law being our tutor until faith comes. One way I have seen this process in operation is in the questions we raise along the way: Can a woman cut her hair? Can I wear a wedding ring, or simple jewelry, or none? Do I have to tithe, or can I give less? Do I have to be at every church service, Bible study and retreat and participate in every other congregation's activities to encourage them, too?

Can I sing standing up front with a choir, only sitting on the front row, or from the back? Can a woman make a comment in class as long as she's sitting down, but if she's standing up front and happens to mention a scripture, is she usurping authority? Or can she never open her mouth in the assembly at all?

The list goes on forever. We want a specific answer, because we want to be right with God. The fact is, we will never do it all right. Even if we had a perfect list of how every detail should be done to please God, we could never follow it. The Good News shouldn't be kept from hungry souls. The Good News is that our Lord and Savior Jesus Christ, Son of God, covers all our blemishes and presents us perfect! It brings tears of joy and wonder and gratitude. How else could I ever come close to my God?

Manuel and I have always functioned as a team in the ministry. We work well together. We complement each other's talents and insights in counseling and teaching. In our specific ministry, I have done a lot of translating, both standing up front and behind the scenes with translating equipment. I have helped my husband write lessons (especially in English). He asks for my input. We pray together about everything from our marriage, personal lives, finances and children to the needs of others and of church leaders in decisions locally and worldwide. We co-teach marriage and parenting classes. I don't have any desire to be up front, but I've learned to be willing to let God use me. I want with all my heart, soul, mind and strength to live a pure and blameless life before him.

Sometimes I have offended people. One time, when we were in a small leaders' group, I started a hymn spontaneously, and a brother got up and walked out. I had no idea what the problem was until someone explained that I had overstepped my boundaries in his opinion. It's okay for both of us to struggle with the issues. I can respect that we can operate out of a clear conscience and come to different convictions. What else is Romans 14 talking about?

I've wasted too much time and energy trying to figure these things out. One year I sat at the Pepperdine Lectures and wept silently through most of the classes. I was so burdened with the issues, I felt we were never going to "get it right." I knew so many precious souls starving for truth. Would solving those issues ever satisfy? Finally, after months of being distracted, I put them aside. The differences will never go away. In all the world and for centuries, people have killed others who did not share their cherished convictions. They have not learned to apply the law of love. It's always a struggle to figure out what to do in each situation, but love will always have a good outcome.

What kind of fruit have we borne in the past century?

A single female missionary was telling me about the congregation she served. The men were concerned about a single woman working in the church and were only comfortable allowing her to teach children's classes. My first thought was of pride and impatience. "I couldn't bear to serve in that environment. Why doesn't she go somewhere where she could do more?" I was immediately humbled when I remembered that Jesus served the least of us. Jesus' living presence is needed in every congregation of believers throughout the world, no matter what its traditions might be.

"he will be faithful to complete it. . . ."
The Lord is faithful. He has blessed my struggling faithfulness in many ways. I now know that part of being faithful is to trust God and be content during the journey, knowing that the good work he began in me will continue to be "carried on to completion until the day of Christ Jesus."

It is beautiful to see how the Lord has woven my childhood, my faithfulness and my questions into the fabric of my life and made me uniquely qualified to serve him in this place and time. The fabric has been beautifully colored by the counsel and example of older brothers and sisters in this loving congregation. God has used the person I have become to enhance their dream of growing into a congregation where first-, second- and third-generation immigrants could worship together despite differing languages and customs. Along the way, I have been prepared to share the love and teaching I have received from them, not only here, but on missionary journeys to Peru. A life-cycle—ministry received, ministry shared.

Julie Kramer Magos has ministered along with her husband Manuel and their six children at the North County Church of Christ, a bilingual congregation in Escondido, California since 1987.

She holds an associate degree in Registered Nursing from Imperial Valley College and has worked in home health nursing.

She grew up on the mission field in Lima, Peru.

14

God at Work in a Woman's Life

Billie Silvey

It was the summer of 1965 when my husband Frank and I came to Los Angeles. The Watts riots had just ended, and the old Pepperdine campus was still under curfew. I felt excited, if a little afraid. Finally, I'd made it to the big city! A security guard met us as we drove onto the campus—a couple of kids fresh from the Texas plains—and told us we had to be in by eight o'clock. Not quite the freedom we'd expected in L.A.

It was a tremendous contrast with Happy, the tiny town in the Texas Panhandle where I grew up. My life there was stable because of three strong roots—family, church and community—that would develop in new and surprising directions while providing stability throughout my life.

Family had always been primary. My parents, sister and I worked, played, worshipped and learned together. My father's mother lived in Happy, and my mother's parents just fifteen miles away, so we spent a lot of time with grandparents, aunts and uncles, and cousins of varying remove. They spread in my mind like a vast family tree, with all the relationships clear and familiar.

The Church of Christ in Happy had begun meeting in my great-grandfather's house outside of town. But by the time I was growing up, it had moved into town and become respectable. My father led singing, and I helped teach Bible classes from the time I was thirteen. The Bible was central to the church, and we studied it and discussed it and argued about it often.

There were 642 people in Happy, so the map of the town was as familiar to me as our family tree. My father owned the weekly newspaper, the *Happy Herald*, and we ran it as a family business. We couldn't afford to hire employees, so the four of us ran equipment, wrote articles and sold ads to get the news to the people. By the time I finished high school, I could run every machine in the shop, though all my knowledge was outdated. Technology had progressed from letterpress to offset while I dreamed of being Lois Lane or Brenda Starr.

These three roots—family, church and community—caused me to grow up with a strong sense of identity, a strong faith, and a strong feeling of connection with, and responsibility toward, the people around me.

My background on my father's newspaper and in public relations at Abilene Christian College helped me get a public relations job at Pepperdine, where I wrote about what was happening on campus. But things were happening on the Pepperdine campus in the mid-60s that were not for public consumption.

My work for Pepperdine had become like the family business of my childhood. I worked nights and weekends to help it succeed, even through events that were a public relations person's nightmare. The location of the Pepperdine campus in South Central Los Angeles, in what was fast becoming a black community, was far from the image the administration wanted to project of a protected environment for young Christians.

Still, it was an education in itself. It taught me about inequities in our society—the poverty, poor schools and general neglect of minority neighborhoods—that seemed unfair and unpleasing to a God who was no respecter of persons. I'd grown up with a strong sense of fairness.

A group of students started a ministry to neighborhood children—offering tutoring, Bible study and sports on Saturday mornings. I was especially dedicated to teaching the children to read, something many local schools were failing at.

About that time, Vietnam moved from a footnote to the front page. It had an even more personal impact when Frank received his draft notice and enlisted in the Navy. We had been married less than three years, and his ship spent over a year of our next two in the Tonkin Gulf. Lonely and worried, I wrote him every day. Gradually, we began to wonder why our nation was involved in a war that seemed so foreign to us and our concerns.

When Martin Luther King was assassinated, I felt especially alone—and self-consciously white in an increasingly black neighborhood. After all, our part of the city had exploded in violence just before we came to California. Would it do the same again?

I had grown up assuming that the way our country did things was the best way possible, but suddenly I found myself questioning a lot of things—especially race relations and the war.

My church family was there for me while Frank was overseas. Bill and Ruby Green, in particular, "adopted" me, and songs like "Peace, Perfect Peace" had a special significance. Even the church wasn't exempt from questioning and change. People were examining the role of the Holy Spirit, and God seemed more active than I had once believed. As comforting as that should have been, I had trouble accepting it. I was strong-willed and wanted to run my own life.

In 1969, my boss in the publicity department drew up a new organizational chart. On it, the position above mine was vacant. I wanted that job. What would it take to get it? Could I take classes or do something to get the broader experience needed to qualify? "No," he told me. "They want a man for that position." It was the first time I had encountered blatant sexual discrimination, and I was angry and confused. How could this be happening at a Christian college? My college?

When Frank came back from overseas and the Navy transferred him to Washington, D.C., I was ready to leave the publicity department and move with him. Not long after we reached Washington, our daughter Kathy was born.

After Frank completed his two-year tour of duty on the East Coast, we were ready to return to Los Angeles. Frank was planning to attend UCLA, and I had applied for a graduate assistantship in English at Pepperdine. The assistantship had already been awarded, but Norvel Young wrote that he could use me with *20th Century Christian* magazine, though they couldn't pay much. We figured to the penny what I'd have to make for us to survive, and when he wrote back, the figure he quoted was exactly what we needed! Clearly God was running things, and this time I was happy to accept his will.

For 24 years I worked for *20th Century Christian*—first as editorial assistant, then assistant editor, then associate editor. It was a wonderful job for a mother, to be able to work out of my house and take care of Kathy, and later our son Robert. I might not have been Lois Lane, but I enjoyed planning issues of the magazine—choosing a theme, reading the relevant Bible passages and background, dividing the topic into articles, and assigning them to writers I knew would handle them well.

I planned issues that had never appeared in publications of Churches of Christ before—Christ and Culture, The Christian and Literature, Christians and Education, Women in Christian Ministry, Creativity, Pollution, and The Touch of the Master in the Inner City. I also planned issues on various books of the Bible, including one that traced the entire Bible story in scripture. What a delight to be paid to study the Bible!

I prayed over each issue, and it was a good thing, too. To pull together the work of a dozen authors from all over the country, edit copy and get it to the printer in Nashville, get it back and read proof—even to choose art and read bluelines—month after month was a daunting task. I called the magazine "the monthly miracle," and I could see God's hand in the way it always came together, often at the last minute. My prayer life grew.

I wrote books and spoke for women's groups and college lectureships. I worked with outstanding writers like Bill Green, J. P. Sanders, Frank Pack, Mary Oler, Carl Spain, Everett Ferguson and Harold Shank.

Joe Barnett, Helen Young and Bill Henegar were kind and encouraging mentors. It was great to help others explore what it means to be a Christian in today's world.

The next step in the organizational chart was editor. But as I worked for one preacher after another, it became clear that that job would never be mine. Again, I faced discrimination and was denied advancement *because* we were Christians. It was frustrating and seemed to have little to do with Christ's nature.

One reason it occurred was that the title "editor" never meant in churches of Christ what it means in other forms of journalism. Traditionally, editors in the church made pronouncements on doctrine and practice. If editor had meant a person who edits copy and plans publications, I doubt that anyone would have been concerned about my editing the magazine. As it was, people were afraid I'd be a woman in church leadership. Other Christian traditions didn't make such distinctions. Harriett Mears at Gospel Light was an editor who made a profound impact on the Christian community and was respected, not penalized, for it. I felt I wasn't trusted to know and do what my experience, education and walk with God had prepared me for.

Painful as it was, I probably could have continued with the magazine indefinitely if the last preacher who was hired over me had seen me as an editorial colleague, rather than his personal secretary. I left my calling of nearly a quarter of a century discouraged and depressed.

About the same time, the congregation at Vermont Avenue—where I had worshipped, taught Bible classes and done benevolence work since coming to Los Angeles thirty years earlier—was experiencing its greatest threat. A new minister seemed determined to drive off members of the congregation, including me. Week after week, I'd cry all the way home from worship. It wasn't until later that we discovered he had been robbing the church and planning to sell the building to a megachurch in the area.

My life, which God had guided in such wonderful ways to that point, was in shambles. I felt betrayed, and I cried out to God in pain. My daughter Kathy suggested that I try worshipping with another congregation. Earlier, she had placed membership at the Culver Palms

Church of Christ, and for some time she had encouraged me to follow her there.

It was hard to leave after 30 years as a part of a small, close-knit congregation. It was hard to give up teaching what was now the second generation of families in South Central Los Angeles. Culver Palms was many times larger than Vermont Avenue, and I doubted that I'd ever get to know so many people.

But Culver Palms has been good to me. Through decades of work in the church in Los Angeles, I had struggled with two serious concerns. Many churches here are small, scattered and turned-inward, focusing on their own needs. They seem intimidated by the city we've been called to serve. In contrast with the South, where churches may have bad reputations to overcome, in Los Angeles we have no reputation at all. Most of the city doesn't even know we exist.

In the New Testament, Jesus' disciples were known as people who "turned the world upside down." We seem more like people who stick our hands in the ocean and pull them out again, leaving no impression at all. How could we get the attention of a city the size of Los Angeles? I put together a weekend seminar called "Making the Church Known in Your Community" and presented it to several different churches, but it was hard to stimulate much interest.

My second concern had to do with the way we do benevolence work. Our Bible class at Vermont Avenue spent three years distributing food to the homeless downtown. Once a month, we'd pack 50 to 100 sack lunches to hand out on the street. People would grab the bags as fast as we could pull them out of the van. When the bags were gone, the people would still be coming. And we knew the next day they'd be hungry again.

Some people seem to think we shouldn't do benevolence work at all. They concentrate on teaching and preaching. Even among churches with a benevolence budget, it's often only a tiny percentage of overall spending. But Jesus' ministry suggests a different emphasis. He taught people, and he helped them. And the way he helped them made more than just a temporary impact. He healed people and sent them home able to care for themselves and their families. Wouldn't it be wonderful to give people in our neighborhoods that kind of help? To make them whole, and send them into the community as productive citizens?

I wrote a proposal to the elders at Culver Palms to put some of the principles I'd been exploring into practice through a position that combined involvement, community outreach and evangelism. They hired me part-time. After decades in Christian journalism, it was amazing to begin a new career in my 50s, working for a local church. God was still guiding my life—and in some pretty surprising ways.

I wrote news articles about various ministries of the church, placed ads in newspapers and yellow pages, hosted special events, joined the Chamber of Commerce, distributed food, and networked with various community groups. We put together a community service committee and looked for ministries that would both help people and attract favorable attention to the church. I enrolled in the master's program in urban ministry at Fuller Seminary.

The community service committee studied what churches were doing in other parts of the country. It was the mid-90s, and there was talk of dismantling the welfare program. How could people with no experience or education be expected to get jobs that paid well enough to support their families? We felt drawn toward offering job preparation classes. Ruth Johnson and I attended an urban ministries conference in Dallas. There we toured Dallas Urban Ministries and met Christians from Memphis Area Community Services—both of which had programs similar to what we were considering.

Ruth, a former junior college president and professor of higher education at Pepperdine, reviewed various materials and chose the Adkins Life Skills Lab curriculum developed at Columbia University. Life Skills Lab is a ten-week program to prepare people to get jobs. It's an expensive program, and Los Angeles doesn't have the huge churches Dallas and Memphis do to support it. We're essentially a mission point ourselves. But Ruth and I prepared a proposal to begin Life Skills Lab, and the elders accepted it.

Such a program would answer both my concerns. It would help the church become known as a force for good in the community, and it would help people, not just with handouts, but with a chance to provide for themselves and their families.

With second-hand computers donated by Bank of America, Culver Palms Life Skills Lab began offering classes in 1997. Since then, we have trained scores of local people to become financially independent. Over the ten weeks a class meets, we see amazing changes in the lives of the students.

One student said she cried when her daughter said she wanted to be like her. Her life had been going nowhere. When she graduated from Life Skills Lab, she got a job, was baptized, got her high school diploma, and began helping teach Bible classes. She enrolled in child guidance classes at West L.A. College, preparing to be a teacher's aide. This spring, we hired her to teach in our computer lab. Now, she's proud that her daughter wants to be like her.

More than 30 volunteers from the congregation and the community work with each Life Skills Lab class. The church is known and respected in the community, and God is glorified. People tell us that we're "doing what a church should do."

I see God's hand in it all. As I meet with various community organizations, I pray that he will lead me to the person he's sent me there to meet. At one luncheon, I sat across from a woman who offered to provide child care for our students while they were in class. At a Chamber meeting, I sat beside a school board member who is now on our advisory board.

Sometimes the point isn't clear. At one of the annual mayor's luncheons, I asked God to show me where to go among the hundreds attending, but I felt no sense of direction. I waited and prayed again. Still no indication. As I turned to leave, two men standing by the door introduced themselves. They were officers of a civic club and asked me to speak for their next meeting.

The meeting was a disaster. I was nervous and didn't speak at all well. But one man was so interested, he literally followed me around the buffet table asking questions. I invited him to the next meeting of our community service committee, and he came. After the next meeting, he stayed for evening service. Eventually, he was baptized.

It's encouraging to visit local businesses and see our graduates at work. It's even more encouraging to look out over the congregation on Sunday morning and see graduates and community people worshipping and serving with us as a result of this ministry.

In the five years I've been with Culver Palms, my job has evolved from an emphasis on community outreach and involvement to directing Life Skills Lab. I currently recruit students and volunteers, raise funds, help graduates find jobs and maintain financial records. Most of the work is new to me, so I've gone back to school to learn how to do it.

The church helps support Life Skills Lab with financial contributions, facilities and a corps of talented volunteers. One group is working to put together partnerships with the larger employers in the area, and another wants to set up an endowment. Last year we incorporated with the elders as our Board of Trustees and an Advisory Board composed of church and community people. We employ a credentialed secondary teacher in the classroom as well as a graduate in the computer lab.

Looking over my life in Christ in the thirty-five years since we moved to Los Angeles, I'm amazed at the opportunities I've had to serve God and his people—first in Christian education, then in Christian journalism, then in a local church, and finally in a faith-based nonprofit. Looking back, I can see how God has led me, even through pain and disappointments, to careers that have brought growth and fulfillment and a greater dependence on him.

Throughout my life, the three basic roots—family, church and community—have held strong. Though I often take them for granted, the confidence I have in the love of my family gives me a firm base from which to reach out to others. Frank and I have been married for thirty-eight years, and now that we're at home by ourselves, we seem to be closer than ever. Kathy and Robert, though grown, manage to show up almost every week, and we're thrilled to see them and catch up with their lives. My mother died last year, and being with her near the end of her life brought back important scenes from my childhood. It also gave me a chance to spend more time with my sister and renew bonds with relatives and friends I hadn't seen in years.

The church, the body of Christ, has been important to me all my life. The concept of the church as a body with many members who have different gifts and use those gifts in concert to do God's work has been made a reality through Life Skills Lab. Many people contribute what they have—money, time, abilities and interests—to make a major outreach effort work in a relatively small church. It's becoming even more evident as the Malibu church and people from Pepperdine join with us as supporters and volunteers.

Community is still important to me, as well. There's a big difference between Los Angeles and Happy, Texas, but I still feel responsible for my neighbors. And who are my neighbors? As Jesus explained in the parable of the Good Samaritan, my neighbors are the people who need my help. Life Skills Lab is the best way I've found to attack the overwhelming problems of the city without being overwhelmed by them. Each person who comes to us represents a family that will leave able to be productive and self-supporting. One family at a time, we're changing our world!

Personally, I feel that there are two limitations on what I should do in the church. I'd never think of preaching or being an elder. But I don't understand why we limit women in other fields. Women should have opportunities to use their talents, contribute and advance. And we should be accorded respect and treated as colleagues in all areas of church work. There is no place in the Lord's body for condescension, power plays or undercutting the contribution women can and do make.

We have too much to do, too far to go, to be the people God would have us be. We have too much to do to win the world for Christ, to serve those in need, and to glorify God through our lives and ministries. It will take all of us for any of us truly to be God's people.

Billie W. Silvey is executive director of the Culver Palms Life Skills Lab in Los Angeles. Formerly associate editor of *21st Century Christian*, she is the author of several books and numerous articles.

She has spoken for women's groups and college lectureships on such topics as time management, urban ministry and biblical studies.

Billie graduated from Pepperdine University and attended Fuller Seminary. She and her husband Frank have two grown children.

15

Rejoice with Those Who Rejoice, Mourn with Those Who Mourn

Amy Bost Henegar

Amanda[1] was born during the fifth month of the pregnancy. She weighed just over one pound. As she lay in the fiberglass bassinet designed to replace the womb—to keep the warmth in and the germs out—her skin was red and looked almost transparent. Her parents were young and had recently decided to turn their lives around. They had vowed to stay away from drugs and had remained clean and sober for about a year. They had married, because they wanted their daughter to be born into a real family. And they had recently rededicated their lives to their faith and become members of a church.

Now they found themselves somewhere they never expected to be—sitting in a Neonatal Intensive Care Unit watching a breathing machine keep their premature infant alive. They were not accustomed to praying. For years they had believed that no God would be interested in hearing their prayers. But now they had no other choice. Their lives had been turned around by the power of God's love. They had faith in God's love and power to heal. Their conviction was real, for they had experienced God's healing power. Now they waited in hope for the same power to heal their helpless baby girl.

The social worker in the N.I.C.U. knew the baby was in critical condition because her kidneys were failing. He had seen many babies like this before, and he knew that if the kidneys didn't begin working within the next twelve hours or so, she wouldn't make it. And he saw the fear in her parents' eyes. When the social worker spoke to them they told him of their faith. They were waiting for a miracle. The social worker hoped that their miracle would come. When he left the bedside, he called the hospital chaplain. The chaplain could support this family. She would understand the family's hope in God on the one hand, and the critical nature of the baby's medical condition on the other.

When I arrived Amanda's parents told me their story. They told about the premature labor pains, the emergency delivery, and their sudden deep love for the tiny baby now clinging to life in the fiberglass bassinet. Then they told me about God. They explained that they believed God could heal the baby. They could tell that I believed too, and they asked me to pray with them. As I prayed for healing, asking God to touch the tiny body and bring function to its kidneys, Amanda's parents joined in silence, and wept.

The next day the baby's mother ran into my office. When she saw me she hugged me, saying, "He did it! God did it!" She explained how the baby's kidneys had started working during the night. "Everyone was so surprised, but I told them God's gonna do it. He's gonna do a miracle!" She was glowing with relief and gratitude. She asked me to pray with her again. We said a prayer of gratitude, thanking God for healing the baby and asking for continued healing and steady growth. Every time I said "Thank you" she echoed the words out loud.

Later that week I received another call from the N.I.C.U. It was Amanda's nurse. The baby had taken a turn for the worse and probably would not make it through the night. She wanted me to come and be with the family. When I arrived in the N.I.C.U. I was ushered to the private room where Amanda's parents were sitting. I walked in and saw them holding the tiny baby. I knew immediately that the baby was dead, for a baby this small could never breathe on its own. Seeing their tear-stained faces, I sat with them and expressed my sorrow.

Amanda's mother looked up from the baby and, once again, asked me to pray. Once again, I led the couple in prayer. This time, I didn't ask for healing and I didn't express gratitude. I prayed a prayer of sorrow, expressing grief, requesting strength and entrusting God with the soul of the one-pound infant.

Later, when I reflected on my experience with this family, I wrote the following words: "I do not have good answers for people who pray for a miracle and a miracle does not come. I do believe that God performs miracles. I don't understand the criteria for who receives the miracle. This, to me, is the hardest of mysteries. But, more important, I believe that God is with us, and somehow this is peace. God is truly there in healing, and God is absolutely there in death. God will go anywhere with us. If I am attempting to demonstrate God's never-ending and prevailing love, I must be willing to be a true companion on the journey—through joy and through suffering."

Hospital Chaplaincy

I have worked as a hospital chaplain for the past four years. My training is similar to that of any other minister. I have a Master of Divinity degree. I did internships with adults, teenagers and children in local churches. But after graduate school I did a chaplaincy residency at a hospital. During that year I worked with people who were suffering from physical illness or personal loss. I spent the year searching the Bible for answers to difficult questions, praying for insight and guidance, and writing about my experience of God and faith in the presence of suffering and pain. My skills for ministry were refined, and my faith was challenged and strengthened.

The spiritual dynamics surrounding suffering are complex. When we are in pain, we sometimes wonder if God is making us suffer to punish us. Or we may think God is letting us suffer to make us strong. Often we believe that our suffering will end if we pray enough. Most of us believe that God has the power to heal, yet we don't always experience healing. Like the biblical character Job, we cry out to God for answers, but clear answers don't always come. The ministry of a hospital chaplain involves walking with people as they wrestle with

God and being a spiritual companion, present through the ups and downs of the journey.

Because I come from a faith group that does not make a practice of employing women as ministers, hospital chaplaincy has led me into some unexpected places. I have preached Sunday sermons, performed weddings and officiated at funerals. When I preach, it is usually in a hospital chapel. The pews are not filled with faithful church members whose names I know. Rather, my congregation is made up of displaced people, brought together by a common lack of stability.

Among the congregants may be a devout Christian woman who is unable to leave the hospital due to the critical nature of a loved one's illness. Or there may be a person who has never set foot in a church building in his life. Perhaps his current crisis has illuminated his need for God, and the chapel service is a first step in that direction. Whatever the situation, those attending a hospital chapel service are usually eager to hear of God's blessings and claim the promises of God's love. The message of the Gospel is the best of news, and it fills me with joy to share it.

When I perform funerals, they usually are for people who do not have a church family and thus do not have a minister they feel close to. Often, they are families I have gotten to know in the hospital. I met the Cox family this way. I was just about to leave for the day when the phone rang in the Pastoral Care Office. The call was an urgent request for a chaplain to come to the operating room where a fifty-five-year-old man had died unexpectedly during surgery. I recognized the man's name. I had prayed with him and his wife earlier in the week.

When I arrived at the surgery waiting room, I encountered a large family. A few people were pacing and looking out the window, others were sobbing loudly, and the man's wife was leaning over a trash can, looking as if she might throw up. I quietly walked into the room and began trying to provide help and comfort.

I spent the next few hours with them. They were devastated, not only because he was gone and at such a young age, but also because it happened so suddenly and they weren't able to say good-bye. The operating room staff and I arranged the body in an empty room so his family could see him before they left the hospital. I escorted family members to see the body and say good-bye. His pregnant daughter-in-law almost fainted. His daughter stared into space and said, "He was the best man."

A few days later they called me and asked me to conduct the memorial service. I was honored to be a part of this sacred moment in their lives.

For hospital chaplains, weddings come in all shapes and sizes. I met Jason and Lisa in the maternity unit. She was in her seventh month of pregnancy. When I told them I was a chaplain, they immediately said, "Do you do weddings?" At that point I had never performed a wedding but I wanted to help them if I could. They explained that, although they already had two children, they had never gotten married. Their third child was on the way, and they felt it was important that they be married before the baby was born. I talked to them for a long time about their faith and about their view of marriage. After some time, I was convinced of their sincerity and agreed that their marriage would be a wonderful gift to the child.

We arranged to have a ceremony in her hospital room later that day. I prepared a simple service, the cafeteria made a little cake, and the nurses located flowers for a small bouquet. With nurses and hospital patients as witnesses, I performed the wedding ceremony for a tearful Jason and Lisa. Later, Lisa explained that she couldn't stop crying because she knew, without a doubt, that God was there participating in their promises to each other.

Other faces fill my mind as I reflect on my hospital experiences. I think of Marcus, the twelve-year-old boy with leukemia who had no family except for an aunt who lived three hours from the hospital. Marcus was in the hospital for almost nine months. I went by his room almost every day to play video games and talk about "The Fresh Prince of Bel Air." I remember when he got so sick he was transferred to the Pediatric Intensive Care Unit. I sat with him and fed him ice chips with sorrow and fear in my heart. But, thanks be to God, I remember the day he was well enough to leave the hospital and go for a bone marrow transplant. I pray that today he's a healthy teenage boy.

I think of Mr. Martinez, telling me with slurred words and distorted facial features about his hopes for health after brain surgery. And I think of Denise and her nine-month-old little boy who was born healthy despite the fact that she was undergoing chemotherapy for breast cancer. I see the pain in her face as she tells me that the cancer has returned and is now in her brain. She wonders if she'll be able to raise her son. Then I think of a woman named Kathy. Her one-year-old daughter had a rare and aggressive brain stem tumor. I remember her looking straight into my eyes as she told me she would sell her soul to the devil if it would save her baby. And I think of the thirty-year-old man with a wife and three beautiful little girls who came into the hospital to have emergency heart surgery. They found his heart covered with cancer and he was dead within two days. I remember his wife moaning in sorrow and her friends surrounding her with loud mournful prayers. I remember the little girls going into the intensive care unit to say good-bye to their father.

And when my heart can hardly take any more, I think of Jesus. "When he saw the crowds he had compassion on them, because they were harassed and helpless, like sheep without a shepherd" (Matt. 9:36). I know these crowds—harassed by the ravages of illness and helpless in the face of unjust suffering. "My soul is overwhelmed with sorrow to the point of death" (Matt. 26:38). I've seen that sorrow—sorrow that feels like death, sorrow that is worse than death. And in Jesus' suffering, in Jesus' participation in our suffering, there is promise. "Never again will they hunger; never again will they thirst. The sun will not beat upon them, nor any scorching heat. For the Lamb at the center of the throne will be their shepherd; he will lead them to springs of living water. And God will wipe away every tear from their eyes" (Rev. 7:16-17). This is the promise—to me, and to them. The promise of hope. The promise of peace.

Where Can I Go From Your Spirit?
Where Can I Flee From Your Presence?

One of the things that drew me to hospital chaplaincy was a desire to get out of the Bible class and into the "real world." I believed God's truth would endure even in the worst circumstances, but I needed to see it happen. I needed to get into the messiness of life and witness the presence of God there. And God has been faithful. In four years of hospital work, I have seen God in many places, people and situations. However, God's presence has never been quite so profound as it was the night I spent with Elizabeth James and her family.

I was on call from 5:00 in the evening until 8:00 the next morning. About 4:45 p.m., I got a call from another chaplain at the Pediatric Intensive Care Unit, letting me know about a family that would probably need some support through the night. The moment I arrived I could tell the situation was serious. The parents were in the child's room and the nurses' station was filled with hospital staff—doctors, nurses, a social worker, a child life specialist and various others. I didn't know much about the situation, only that the nine-month-old girl had been healthy until two days earlier, and now she was not expected to make it through the night. I went into the room and introduced myself to the baby's parents.

The baby was lying on a bed in the middle of the room. She did not look terrible—just swollen, with a number of tubes in her body. She was breathing with the help of a machine. I stood with the parents for a while, looking at the little girl and asking occasional questions. I learned that the parents had been married for one year, that their anniversary was the coming Sunday, that they were part of a non-denominational Christian church, and that they were worried about their three-year-old son who was also sick, but in another hospital, not understanding where his parents had gone.

Taped above Elizabeth's head were three pictures. One was of her brother. The second was of the mother in a hammock with a child on each side. Elizabeth's mother, Michelle, was beautiful. She had long brown hair and a pale face. She looked quite young, and I found out later that she was only 20 years old. Her husband, Brad, was 22. They were an attractive couple and a beautiful family. The third picture was of the four of them, with little Elizabeth in the middle with a bow on top of her head, a piece of hair sticking straight up, and a big smile on her face.

After a while I went to the nurses' station to get more information. The social worker told me that the little girl had R.S.V.—a respiratory condition that is extremely serious for premature infants but rarely affects babies of this age and health. She had been taken to the doctor with a cough on Tuesday, had stopped breathing in the doctor's office, and had been helicoptered to the hospital.

Wednesday she had done okay, and the medical team thought she would make it, but today they performed C.P.R. on her three times, and the doctors were worried about her neurological status. They were waiting for neurological test results. Currently they were preparing her to receive dialysis, which they saw as a last-ditch effort to remove toxins from her body.

I went back into the room with the parents, and we sat in a corner watching two doctors and two nurses move an IV line from her shoulder to her leg. We spoke as we watched. They said that it felt like a bad dream, and their worst fears seemed to be coming true. At one point the mother said, "I trust God, that if he has to take her.... I mean I know he will do what's best.... But I just can't imagine doing it." I asked her what she couldn't imagine. She said, "Going home without her, and going through her stuff. I just couldn't do it."

The medical team encountered problems preparing Elizabeth for dialysis. Tension seemed to be rising, and we saw more bloody towels and new instruments. I wondered if it was difficult for Brad and Michelle to witness such a procedure, but they seemed fine. They had no interest in leaving their baby's side. Finally, however, the nurse asked them to leave for a little while. I told them I would stay in the room and let them know of any developments. Michelle went to the room where at least fifteen family members had gathered, and Brad left to check into their room at the Ronald McDonald House.

I stood by the door, watching the physicians work. Not ten minutes had passed when I noticed the doctor doing what looked like chest compressions. I was stunned as I saw this tiny person's chest being pressed so forcefully by this large man. There had been no announcement, no one had screamed, "Her heart is stopping!" There had been no outward indication that things had just gone very wrong.

But I quickly realized that they had, and that the medical professionals in the room were doing everything they could to save her. A bell was ringing throughout the unit, a light was flashing above the door, and a crowd of doctors and nurses descended on the room. I stepped back and watched in awe.

A few minutes later, a nurse said, "Where are the parents?"

"I can get them," I answered and ran down the hall to the family room. I grabbed Michelle and told the family to call the Ronald McDonald House and get Brad.

When Michelle and I got back to Elizabeth's room, things were a little calmer but everyone was still there. We stood by the door in silence, Michelle staring at her baby. I could feel a unique strength in her. It was like she needed to be strong because she was this child's mother, and she had to use all her strength to fight for her baby. She stared straight through the people, past the equipment, at the baby, as if she were looking into Elizabeth's eyes, encouraging her to hold on. Finally she asked me, "Did they have to do C.P.R. again?"

"Yeah, I think so," I replied.

A few minutes later the baby's grandfather came to the room. He put his arm around Michelle and after a couple of seconds he began to pray.

The next couple of hours were a blur of activity. I spent most of the time outside Elizabeth's room with her parents, and at times her grandparents, watching the doctors and nurses continually working. At one point everyone had stepped out except Michelle. I was standing behind her with my hand on her back. She made a noise that sounded like a laugh and a cry. I asked her what she was thinking about.

"I was just thinking about her playing. Just Tuesday in the doctor's office she was playing."

"What does she do that you are remembering?" I asked.

"You take your gum and put it between your front teeth so that she can see it, and she really gently reaches up and touches it and then she laughs and laughs."

"And she was doing that in the doctor's office on Tuesday?"

"Yeah."

183

"What a sweetheart."

"She's the happiest baby."

Brad had returned and joined the conversation. "Yeah, it has always been the one thing you can count on. No matter how crazy everything else was, you could always count on Elizabeth waking up with a smile."

Michelle then said, "It's almost like it was too perfect. You know? I had been thinking it was so perfect that something bad was going to happen."

"Yeah, I remember you saying that," Brad answered.

As the hours passed, I found myself drawn to the pictures above the bed. That beautiful baby with the big smile. She reminded me of so many little girls I knew. A number of my friends had one-year-old daughters, and Elizabeth could just as easily be one of them. She could be my daughter. There was nothing that explained why this was happening to them and not to me. They were being good parents to a healthy, happy baby, just like I would be, just like my friends are. Feeling overwhelmed, I asked God to save this baby. I told him I didn't understand why this kind of thing has to happen at all.

Although they had been able to stabilize her after the first Code Blue, the threat of another one was very real, and Michelle was constantly watching Elizabeth's blood pressure on the monitor. At one point I saw that her blood pressure was dropping, and I got a feeling of dread in my stomach. I didn't want to go through another round of C.P.R. But her blood pressure did drop, and they did have to do C.P.R. again. Brad, Michelle, Michelle's dad and I all stood at the door and watched as the doctor did the chest compressions. Brad kept saying, "Come on baby, you can do it baby," quietly as he watched. Michelle whispered, "Oh God, please God, please save my baby, please Jesus." Once again they got her blood pressure back up, but the nurse informed me that each time would be more difficult than the time before.

Finally things seemed to calm down. They were still trying to get her on dialysis and seemed to be making slow progress. I told the family that I was going to leave for a little while, but I would be back soon. My feet were killing me and I needed to eat, so I told the nurse to page me if anything changed before I returned. I left the hospital and went home to change clothes and get some food. I hadn't been home fifteen minutes when I was paged. The nurse told me that they were performing C.P.R. again, and I told her I would be there as soon as possible. I put on a warm sweater, comfortable pants and running shoes, knowing that I had a long night ahead of me, and returned to the hospital.

The scene had changed since I left. They had given up on the dialysis; the machines and the dialysis nurses were gone. Brad and Michelle were in the room with Elizabeth, and a large group of relatives was standing in the hallway outside the room. Their pastor had come. He was a tall man with curly hair who looked in his late 30's. He was wearing jeans and a T-shirt from some sort of Christian camp, and had a silver loop earring in one ear. He was standing with the family waiting for news.

Before long the doctor explained to Michelle and Brad that Elizabeth's heart was in the process of dying. She was being given an enormous amount of adrenaline to keep her heart going, but it was still stopping. He told them that the chest compressions would start the heart for a short period of time, but that it would just stop again. "At this point," he said, "the chest compressions are really more abusive than helpful." He then suggested that they not do C.P.R. if her blood pressure were to drop again. "That way you can hold her," he said, with pain in his face.

"I want to hold her," Michelle said. Everyone helped to quickly arrange the cords and tubes, and put the baby in Michelle's arms.

The pastor tapped me on the shoulder. He asked if it would be okay for him to pray, and I assured him that he should. I had not offered to pray as I usually do, because they had prayed so freely on their own, and I had assumed that the pastor would pray with them at some point. I was glad he was going to.

He went over to where the mother was holding the baby. The father was standing next to her, and two sets of grandparents surrounded them. Everyone had tears streaming down their faces, and Michelle whispered to Elizabeth. The pastor stood behind and over the whole group and put his arms around them. He told them to keep talking to her as he prayed. His prayer was beautifully pastoral—a cry to God on behalf of these grieving people.

After the prayer I brought him my Bible. He started reading psalms, again encouraging the family to continue their words to Elizabeth. Because their own pastor was leading them in prayer and scripture meditation, I was able to stand back and observe. The scene was poignant—dying baby, mom, dad, grandparents, pastor, aunts and uncles, great aunts, nurses—all with tears on their faces, everyone holding each other and focusing on the whispered words of the parents to their baby.

My eyes were dry until I heard the pastor read the words that providentially had been on my mind all day long: "Be still and know that I am God; I will be exalted among the nations, I will be exalted in the earth. The Lord Almighty is with us; the God of Jacob is our fortress" (Psalm 46:10-11). We were still. Not because we chose to be, but because we had to be. We could do nothing more. As human beings we had reached the end of our capabilities. And somehow, in the mystery of this beautiful and horrifying event, God was being exalted. I saw it. I knew it.

The scripture reading continued as Michelle and Brad alternated holding the baby and her blood pressure slowly dropped. I was called to the adult intensive care unit to be with the family of a 35-year-old man who was dying because the flu had turned into viral pneumonia. I was back, however, by the time the family asked to see the doctor. The parents were considering turning off the respirator.

The doctor walked into the room, and Michelle looked straight at him and said, "So she's going to die anyway?"

The doctor said, "Yes."

"Then," she replied, "I don't want her to suffer any more."

The doctor nodded and left the room to make the necessary arrangements. The pastor said another prayer with the whole family holding each other. Michelle was on one side of the bed and Brad on the other, both leaning over Elizabeth.

After the prayer, Michelle put her face on Elizabeth's bare tummy and cried as she spoke. "I'll never forget you," she said. "My baby was fine, my baby was fine. I would do anything for you. I would die for you. I never thought God would do this."

This continued, and Elizabeth was never taken off the respirator. The doctor and the respiratory therapist stayed by the room, but the time never came. Elizabeth's blood pressure dropped slowly but consistently, and it was clear that she would not suffer long. Brad had been quiet—crying some and praying softly, but not as demonstrative as Michelle. At one point, however, his older brother, a nice-looking man in a suit, hugged him. Brad broke down in his brother's arms. They stood holding each other and sobbing.

Finally, at midnight, the monitor showed Elizabeth's blood pressure to be at 0. Her heart was beating very seldom. The doctor examined her and told Brad and Michelle that she was gone. They thanked the doctor and the nurses, kissed her one last time, and gathered their belongings.

In the hallway outside the room, the rest of the family waited. Michelle's 18-year-old sister was sitting in a chair at the nurses' station. She looked pale and distraught. She had never gone into the room. A relative tried to comfort her, but she insisted that she was fine. Another family member looked at me and said, "This is the most heartbreaking thing I have ever seen."

While Brad and Michelle were gathering their belongings, I asked if they would like us to remove the tubes and let them have some time alone with Elizabeth.

"She's not here," Michelle said, and they walked out of the room. Three steps into the hallway Michelle melted to the floor, and Brad and her parents surrounded her. She knelt with her face toward the ground crying, "I want my baby, I want my baby. I never thought God would do this, I never thought God would do this." Her cry was a lamentation—a cry to God from a mother whose child was gone. "A voice is heard in Ramah, mourning and great weeping, Rachel weeping for her children and refusing to be comforted, because her children are no more" (Jer. 31:15).

They stayed for ten minutes or so, until Michelle was composed enough to be led out of the hospital. I followed them out and said good-bye. After they left, I thanked the nurses and the doctor. Then I went up to the adult intensive care unit and found that the 35-year-old man was not doing well, but they did not need me at the moment. I went down to my office, called my husband and told him the story, and went to sleep. I woke up about 5:30 a.m. to check on the I.C.U. As I left the office thinking about everything that had happened the night before, I looked outside. It had been raining. I stepped out and breathed in the cool, damp air.

The rain gave me a profound feeling of comfort. I was over-whelmed with the knowledge that God was here. The rain communicated that the world was different this morning. Yesterday was sunny, but this morning, it was cold and cloudy. God knew that today was not a sunny day. It was a cold, damp, sad day. And my heart was consoled.

"Blessed are those who mourn, for they shall be comforted" (Matt. 5:4).

Note

1. All names have been changed to maintain the anonymity of those involved.

Amy Bost Henegar grew up in Los Angeles. She holds the B.A. from Pepperdine University in humanities and the M.Div. from Fuller Theological Seminary.

She did her pastoral education residency at Loma Linda University Medcal Center and currently serves as staff chaplain at Lenox Hill Hospital in Manhatten and interim children's minister at the Manhatten Church of Christ.

She is married to Matt, and is the mother of Aidan John Henegar, born in July 2001.

16

The Way of Women
in Churches of Christ

Sherrylee Woodward

Minister. Looking at the word I had just written in the blank marked occupation, Tevye's cry from the musical, *Fiddler On The Roof,* floated around in my head: "Unthinkable!" How could I be a minister in the Church of Christ? We don't have women ministers, do we? How was it then, that in the year 1989, I was one?

I had often described myself as a minister's daughter, niece, sister, cousin and wife. By seventh grade my teachers knew I wanted to marry a minister and do mission work. It did not seem strange to me to find myself on the field as a missionary at the age of nineteen. My dowry, I joked, was three supporting congregations and elderships.

What were those elders thinking? Even I knew better than to let too many people know my age back in 1971! But then, I was not really a missionary; I was a missionary's wife. Our elders watched and teased that they had gotten two for the price of one. Something was wrong with that equation, I mused, but I did not spend a lot of time trying to figure out what. I had no job description, yet I reported and was accountable to our supporting church for the way I lived my days and spent our budget. I loved every minute of it.

Mark and I thought about our work in a different way from some of the mission couples we knew. We thought of ourselves as a unit. I had married a missionary, a mission field and a mission team. He had married a woman who was incapable of being left out of life's most important matters. In becoming one with Mark Woodward, I knew we would become one in our life's goal: to tell the story of Jesus. In his becoming one with me, he knew we were in this thing we called missions together.

In missions we created a world where we could come into friendly relationships with people who did not know the Lord, baptize them into Christ, and make them disciples. That work happened around our coffee table, at the zoo, at Camp Gemuenden and in a group of chairs arranged in a circle around the Lord's table. I often cradled a baby in my lap. Mark sometimes put a toddler down for a nap while I continued the conversation over a second cup of coffee. He preached the sermon from the pulpit, and I continued it around the dinner table. We reminded each other that he could help clean up the kitchen, and that I should help create the curriculum. Neither of us would rest until all the work for the day was finished. Laundry or the next lesson outline, it was both of our work.

We edited each other, got in each other's way sometimes, and eventually learned to work well together as parents, teachers and missionaries. We learned to love each other as ourselves, and that included loving each other's opinions, teaching styles and search in the scriptures. We still work at it, treasuring the process of life and ministry together. Our goal and our vow is to hold each other up to honor as we live lives that are worthy of our calling.

Asking Questions and Finding My Voice

Discovering my voice within the church started at an early age. I spoke up in Ladies' Bible Class at age four, so I'm told, if Dad's questions went a few seconds unanswered. Volunteering for church work was part of my early life: dusting pews, folding bulletins, visiting the hospital to pray over the sick, baking a cake for Sunday dinner and the visiting preacher. I absorbed my Dad's sermon point: "if everyone in this church were just like me, what kind of church would this church be?" It was obvious to me that the women in my church did not preach or hold the office of elder, but it never occurred to me to be less active or less responsible, or even less vocal, in my Christianity than my brother was. He spoke at chapel at Bible Camp. I planned the lakeside devotions, complete with candles. Sorting out the sermon points and discussing the latest church program were normal Sunday dinner conversation. Dad was the preacher, and asking for "more proof" was the kids' prerogative. Visiting preachers, missionaries and relatives were never protected from our questions. When I did not like what was going on at church, I was encouraged to go talk with the elders. Elders were people in the church I grew up knowing, liking some more than others, and knowing they had faults and family problems just like everyone else. By the time I was 17, I had no problem approaching them with my dreams of an All Gulf Coast Youth Rally. The elders encouraged me to get to work on it.

I was also often admonished with I Peter 3:4. Better known by now as a cheerleader than the quiet type, I wrestled with the question of whether I could have a gentle and quiet spirit with an active mind always coming up with more ideas of what our church, youth group or camp might be doing next. I tried to reconcile the gentle Sarah who called Abraham "Lord" with the imperious Sarah who ordered up a pregnancy and then dismissed the result from her household with Abraham's blessing. Can God use, can God like the young woman I knew myself to be? Daddy was heard to say with a smile, "Sherrylee's going to have to find herself a really strong husband." That was probably about when I began to dream of starting the first Church of Christ nunnery!

More questions surfaced. During those tender devotions of the late sixties youth rallies, my crowd first began to wonder about applying the pattern for church worship, order and leadership when the church was not "in church." Could we sing the folk song, "Go Tell It On the Mountain," around the campfire with a guitar? When we sing about Jesus being born in that song, is my heart worshipping? (Mine was!) Then was I sinning because of that guitar?

I can talk within our Bible discussion circle until we pray, and then I must be silent. Or maybe I can pray out loud so long as I don't lead (start or finish) the prayer. Even "at church" the principles I grew up cherishing began to look a little arbitrary. I can call out a hymn number if the song leader asks for suggestions, but I cannot start the song—unless he goofs on the first measure, and then I can carry the lead and help him get back on pitch. I can sing out loud, but I cannot pray out loud. Men can sing songs written by a woman, but they cannot pray prayers voiced by a woman. I could read scripture in Bible class, but not during the worship.

It was interesting that the professor who taught my Dad and the other "preacher boys" homiletics at David Lipscomb College in those days was a woman. So a woman taught Dad how to build and deliver a sermon? Well, those were war years, I was told.

And I worried about those angels in 1 Corinthians 11. As a new bride in Oxford, Mississippi, I began tying my hair back with a ribbon with the ends hanging down, (my "veil") so the angels watching would know I respected my husband and placed myself under his authority. I also wondered whether those veiled Corinthian women knew how to pray silently. And why would one prophesy silently? Why would they need to be veiled if this were Ladies' Bible Class?

On campaigns what was my role in teaching an unbeliever? If my campaign partner were weak in the scriptures, should I be quiet or jump in and help? And if I did, would I seem to be taking over? What if I were better at personal work than the guy I'm paired with? What if most women were better at public prayer than most men? The joke in some circles was that God had given leadership of the church to men because it was the only way to get men into the church. Anyone on the mission field knows the difficulty in reaching the men of the families with the gospel. The wives, sisters and mothers often come to Christ first.

Planting a new church in northern Germany with our mission team, we reveled in the opportunity to start fresh and let the Bible speak to the new converts. All-church business meetings were fun and lively with all the members present. The single women had great ideas and hearts that longed to be heard. Ten years later, we missionaries moved away and, to our surprise, the German church asked the women to stay away from the business meetings. The rationale was that because the women were so strong-minded and capable, the men were reluctant to take responsibility. The women, most of them mothers by now, were overworked and frustrated, and the men were resentful. It seemed the best decision at the time. Had the women usurped something? Had the men been too passive?

The Spirit of Submission
By the end of the seventies, Mark and I found our young family back in the States, trying to adjust to Christian married life in the Bible Belt. Reverse culture shock brought everything into super sharp focus, and rethinking life seemed a daily challenge. No longer a missionary but a mother of three, I missed my sense of being used by God for a specific purpose. We raised our little kingdom of God at home, I went back to school, and Mark found a teaching position at Oklahoma Christian University that would allow us to continue being involved in missions. My personal musings and searchings about my place in congregational worship and body life found some tentative resolution.

I had long ago decided to skip the veil. The angels watching over me and witnessing the mystery of God's grace on display in my life surely knew by now that I live to please my Lord and my husband. I bring them both glory by my life and demeanor. Wearing a hat does not strengthen that witness.

A submissive spirit shows itself in handling the problems of life with grace and contentment, not by speaking softly or seldom. The gift of talking is wonderful when God uses it to connect people with him and his children. Telling the truth in love about life, about God and about reality became my goal.

Mark and I had not yet heard the term mutual submission, but it was obvious to us that if he would give up his life daily for me and love me like his own body, then he was showing submission to me also out of reverence to God. Later as Mark prepared to be an elder, we studied leadership, authority and service in the church and came to some further conclusions.

We are in submission to God, and were created out of the abundance of his love and for his glory. We are in submission to Christ. He bought us and set us free. We owe him everything.

I am in submission to my husband. I was created for him, because it was not good for him to be without me. He needs all that I am. My challenge is to find ways to give all that brings glory and honor to him and to Christ.

Mark is in submission to me. He loves me as Christ loves the church, that is, sacrificially. We each put the other's needs before our own, and we celebrate our belonging to Christ and to each other. Our bodies are not our own.

We also are in submission to our children. Their needs must be met during the years when they are dependent on our selflessness. One of their needs is to know that they are not the center of our universe—God and his church are.

We submit to our elders. They pray for us, and God has made them to be our shepherds. I need to cooperate with the vision God gives them for our congregation.

We submit to our parents and honor them always. We submit to our fellow members of our church family—serving, bearing with, honoring and building up each other in the Lord. We are in submission even to that rude clerk at the store, to treat her as we would treat the Lord.

As we studied the scriptures, trying to define leadership for elders, I began to see an entirely different picture. God's world has hierarchy all right, but Jesus came to turn things inside out in true metanoia of the world's paradigm. In God's church we lead by serving; we exercise authority in love and gentleness; we change things through teaching and prayer; and we lead by surrendering our will and doing what is best for others in God's will. All power and rule is God's, never ours.

Elders don't act as lords over the church in a worldly way and no Christian husband acts as lord over his wife in a pagan way. Christ shows us how to wash each other's feet. Studying the word of God regarding Christian elders impacted my view of what godly leadership looks like in the home and in marriage.

The first three chapters of Ephesians began to mold my thinking about men and women working together in God's church. Paul teaches that Christ came to abolish the walls of separation. Everything and everyone is to come under the headship of Christ. In that frame of reference, all power struggles cease, and God's people in God's church demonstrate to all creation God's nature of harmony, unity, grace and sacrificial love. What happens in the church and in Christian marriage is a new thing that has never been seen before, by people or by angels, the heavenly hosts or the powers that be. This new age in which God's Holy Spirit indwells both men and women is a precursor of the way things will be in the new heaven and the new earth. Men and women don't use each other in the Way Christ came to reveal. Men and women treasure the fact that each can be used by God to display the lavish richness of his love, which is Christ in us. We value each other in a totally new way.

The nature of God, whose Spirit indwells us, incorporates both maleness and femaleness, according to the story of creation. When man and woman come together in marriage, it is a wonderful example of Christ, the church and the divine. What man and woman discover in the struggles of a loving marriage, and what the bride of Christ, the church, discovers in loving relationship with the Christ are God's ways of revealing his nature more fully. A man alone in life is not generally a good thing, nor is a community without the headship of Christ. The creation story teaches us that Adam found the entire creation wanting until God created Eve.

God charged them both with the responsibility of subduing and caring for creation. Men leading and making decisions about churches without the input of women's counsel, wisdom and insight would seem out of character for God's plan for his church. The order in God's church is not the world's order. It is still a man's world. It is not a man's church.

To that church, God gives many gifts. Everyone is to use his or her gifts for the building up of the whole. Burying our talents is not pleasing to God. But Paul reminds the Corinthian church that, when we come together, some rules of propriety apply. Just because Corinthian women are joint-heirs with their husbands in Christ and have been given spiritual gifts, they should not lose their sense of submissiveness or flaunt their freedom in Christ in the face of cultural norms.

Servants and Fellow-Workers in God's Church
Peter teaches that being a daughter of Sarah means my life speaks louder than my words, especially with my husband. If I want to be beautiful into old age, I will pay attention to the inside more than the outside. A reverent, chaste woman with a quiet spirit who seeks refuge in God and chooses to do right, can face the terror of decay without looking horrible or feeling terrified. Decorate your life with good deeds, not with material things, and continue to walk by faith and believe the promise, just as Sarah did. A woman whose sense of personhood comes from God need not be afraid of taming her own will to serve others. It is the imperious Sarah who can call Abraham her lord without fear. She has learned who is in control of her life and future.

The apostles taught that men should pastor and teach the church and hold the positions of authority. Because Adam sinned, sin and alienation come to all men; but through the one man, Christ, forgiveness and reconciliation follow. God honored man by choosing manhood for Jesus. Because Eve was deceived, women do not have authority in the churches. Eve became the transgressor, but the God of paradox and surprise honored women by choosing that Jesus should come into the world through her. Bearing children is a holy thing God allows to happen in our bodies. We share with Mary the process by which salvation came to God's creation. I do not pretend to have answers for all the questions that have arisen about this scripture (1 Tim. 2). I do think the alternative reading: "through the birth of the child," makes more sense in the context. Paul Stookey's words, "...woman takes her life from man, and gives it back again, oh there is love," echo often in my ears (I Cor. 11:12). God is the God of wonderful synergy.

I often wonder why Satan tempted Eve, dangling the tempting carrot of being like God, knowing good from evil, and being wise.

Sometimes I think God knows we women yearn so much for godliness that we will almost always go about attaining it the wrong, quick, easy way, just as Eve did. Did God tie us to birth and nurturing to keep us firmly rooted in service instead of spiritual ambition?

The apostles taught that women should be busy managing their households, using their homes to show hospitality (the early church often met in women's homes), rearing their children and teaching other women to love their families. Women are encouraged to fill their lives with good deeds for others. Widows who could devote themselves to the church are encouraged not to remarry but to make Christ their first love. The seven daughters of Philip were known as prophets, and the women in 1 Corinthians 11 were praying and prophesying in the assembly. Paul called several women his fellow workers in the kingdom, and Phoebe was a minister of God's church in Philippi.

Women are to be servants of the church, ministers of the church, fellow-workers alongside even the apostles in the church, using their homes to host God's church, prophesying and praying in the church, managing households, rearing children, showing respect to their husbands and never using their freedom in Christ to wrest authority from the evangelists, elders or recognized teachers for the church.

A spirit of submission and gentle graciousness toward others is the mark of every Christian, but it seems that the early Christian women needed special reminders to remember God's order of creation, even in the church where all things were new. God, Christ, man, woman. God heads Christ, Christ heads man, man heads woman. God in Christ, Christ in God, Christ in men and women. Man finds himself in woman; woman gives her life to man. Man gives his life for woman. Men and women in Christ. Singles in brotherly, sisterly relationship to each other in Christ. Fellowship. Body. Community. Family. Things don't happen here as they do in the world, where the strong dominate the weak. Dominion is for God alone, and God's dominion is exercised in perfect, self-giving love.

Who stands up, who speaks through a microphone, who passes trays, who reports to the church what God has done, who counts the money, who words the prayers, who reads the Word, who sings to the church a word of encouragement, who speaks words to build up the church, who has a hymn, who by reason of practice discerns good from evil in difficult situations, who dreams dreams of what a congregation could be doing next, who prays for the sick, who encourages the grieving, who cares for the widows and orphans, who tells the story of Jesus, who admonishes whom?

Servants in God's church do these things as the elders oversee. And servants have no authority at all.

I direct a missions ministry together with my husband. We both serve on the Board of Directors of the "Let's Start Talking" ministry which grew out of our work with students in the early 1980s at Oklahoma Christian University. We have designed a program in which English-speaking Christians of all ages can go into any city of the world and read and discuss the gospel of Luke with one person at a time in conversation sessions. People come looking for help with their English. They go away with a new interest in God's word and God's people. Some of these people have hearts that are open to the word and to the love of their Christian reading partner. Such people come to Christ.

In 1980 we trained ten people to go to two cities. In 2000 we trained 300 Christians who worked in 70 mission projects in 24 countries. Missionaries request these LST teams to help them in their outreach. In recent years we began our FriendSpeak program, because churches here at home were asking for help in reaching out to internationals in U.S. cities.

Presently, LST teams are training weekly in at least 30 states or provinces in North America. I spend most of my days thinking up ways, implementing plans and developing materials to help Christians here in the U.S. and in Canada know how to share their faith more effectively with international people. I help missionaries discover how to use and follow up this kind of outreach. I share what we have learned through the years with freshmen, elders, ministers, grandmothers and teens.

I devise devotional themes, write training materials, encourage mission committees, recruit elders, raise funds, develop conflict resolution games, speak to church groups, select mission sites with which to work, train interns in missions, report to contributors, elders and mission committees, teach teams to verbalize their faith, and evaluate outreach and follow-up efforts in evangelization.

I teach, encourage, oversee, manage, pray with and for, mentor, inspire, recruit, regulate, organize, plan worship times for, and have enormous fun with Christians of all ages who love missions. I minister. I serve. I am in subjection to a great many people as I do so. I trust God will use me up, throw me away and then recycle me in glory. I am a woman in the Churches of Christ.

Sherrylee Johnson Woodward is an executive director of the Let's Start Talking ministry with her husband Mark. The ministry recruits, trains and sends out teams to do short-term mission work.

Sherrylee has been married for 31 years, the first eight of which she worked as a missionary in Germany, where her three children were born.

After moving to Oklahoma City in 1979, she taught German to K-12 graders in a private school and served as educational director for the Dayspring Church of Christ.

Sherrylee has worked full time with the LST ministry since 1989. She holds a B.A. in English from Oklahoma Christian and has co-authored the book, *Let's Start Talking: A Strategy for World Evangelism*.

God Willing

Lucile Todd

Looking back on my earlier years, I wonder if what I considered "coincidences" were the result of my decision to read the Bible as if I had never heard a sermon, read an article or attended a Sunday school class. As I continued to read and pray, my desire to grow closer to the Lord increased to overflowing.

I longed to discuss my search with someone who would understand, but I was often thwarted by the teaching around me. In the church assembly I could hardly be still because of the fire in my soul. Yet there was no avenue to speak of my discovery in public worship or even in Bible classes. I often thought of the two disciples who were joined by Jesus on their way to Emmaus. After he left, they said to each other, "Were not our hearts burning while he talked with us on the road?"

I was in my forties and was teaching speech, drama and English literature in a high school in Houston, Texas. I had heard people speak disdainfully of the Holy Spirit movement, but I had not explored the literature about it. I learned about the Holy Spirit through my own experiences of his operation in my life.

About this time a friend called to set up an appointment with Norvel Young, then president of Pepperdine University. The friend and Dr. Young came to my home, and Dr. Young wasted no time getting to the point of his visit. He said in essence, "Pepperdine College is at a crucial point. We have not had a dean of women in three years, and the accreditation committee told us during their last visit that they would take our accreditation away if we did not fill that position by fall." It was the spring of 1960.

I replied, "You are about three years too early. I cannot accept your invitation, but thank you for your consideration."

Return to College

In my heart and mind, I yearned to return to university for a Ph.D. so I could again teach in a small college. I had taught at Trinity University in San Antonio, Texas during World War II. During those years a woman did not ask her husband to leave his position as vice-president of his company to relocate because his wife was offered a job somewhere else. My husband, Bill, had already had to leave me and our two small children to serve his country in the U. S. Navy. Upon his return home, he had rebuilt his professional life, and his hard effort was paying off. He had a good position with his company.

While he was in combat I, who had never earned a nickel in my life, had to face the possibility of his not returning. Bill was stationed on a warship in the South Pacific at a time when Japan was sinking our ships as fast as they came out of the harbor. At first, in order to deal with my fear, grief and loneliness, I would ask a neighbor to sit with my children, and I would ride a city bus to the end of the line and back. As I rode I listened to the people on the bus talk about their problems. It eased the pain in my heart to realize that other people were "in the same boat."

Some of the younger women went home to their parents, but my father was a gospel preacher in places where recovery from the Great Depression had not yet taken place. Besides, going home was not a long-term solution for me, because the year before Bill was called up for service, we had bought our first home. I decided to complete my education, since I had left college at the end of my junior year. Upon reflection I can see that God was faithful, even when I wasn't—during those periods when I felt abandoned or put upon.

I went to the local USO and offered my services as a book reviewer. In exchange I asked the manager to select a suitable service couple with a child to live in our home with me and our children and help pay the house note. We had some savings I could use for tuition. A private Christian school accepted our son, Bill, for first grade and our daughter, Kay, for kindergarten even though she was a bit young. I wanted my son to have a man in his daily activities, and his teacher was a fine man.

Somehow I managed the necessities, balancing my college class load with as normal a life as I could maintain. I was home from class when the children came home from school. After playtime and our evening meal, we would do the bedtime routine, and then I would study. At first, my schedule was to study all night one night and until midnight on alternate nights for three months. It took twelve months to complete the Bachelor of Arts degree at Trinity University.

Since I already had been recognized for my work in speech and drama in the city, I was offered a teaching position at Trinity with the stipulation that I would begin work immediately on my master's degree. I enrolled in St. Mary's University in San Antonio for evening and Saturday classes. When there was no sitter available, I took the children to class with me. In the summer they visited their grandparents, and I stayed in the dorm.

At Trinity, a Methodist and Presbyterian university, I created chapel services using drama. How wonderful to be able to use all my talents in work for the Lord! I chose a student with a good speaking voice to read the Scriptures as other students in Biblical costumes pantomimed the story. When word got around on campus that it was drama day in chapel, the auditorium was always full.

After five years at Trinity, I resigned to accept a teaching position in the school our children attended. This new position gave me more control over my schedule and professional and family commitments. My husband and I didn't talk about the Pepperdine offer. It was not in my plans, but during that summer of 1960, J. P. Sanders, the academic dean of Pepperdine, called me every week. He would phone "just to see how you are doing," with no mention of the offer.

Finally, by September, my husband said, "You don't turn down a job without first looking at it." I protested that I couldn't, in good conscience, spend the college's money on plane fare when I knew I wasn't going to accept the position. "That's their problem, not yours," he said.

I didn't want to make the trip until school began and I could see the students, but deep down I was beginning to feel interested. It was the latter part of September when I boarded a plane for California. I carried a stack of test papers from my own classes and planned to grade them during the short trip.

People at Pepperdine were cordial and gracious. I slipped away from the welcoming committee and wandered around campus, looking at the students and listening to them. It was only then that God "laid his hand on me," and I knew that the students needed me. How he would work it out was a mystery to me, but I signed a letter of intent for the accreditation committee in Dean Sanders's office. I have often wondered, Were people at Pepperdine praying for a dean of women?

I went back home to Bill and our children and later visited my parents. Late one afternoon as I watched the sun set I prayed, "Father, I want to go, but I don't see how it is possible."

In November my husband came home from his office and said, "I've turned in my company car and office keys!"

A Missionary Journey

I told Dean Sanders that I couldn't be on campus until the first of April, since I had promised the junior class I would direct their class play in February. He assured me it would be acceptable. My husband sold some of our furnishings and purchased a new car and a road map. Late in March we closed the door to our lovely new home and told our parents goodbye. Then we went to Abilene Christian College to see our children before heading West on what to us was a missionary journey.

My husband had no idea what he would do to earn a living in Los Angeles. Salaries in Christian schools, especially for women, covered only the bare essentials in those days. We were, however, about our Father's business!

We lived in a lovely old Spanish style house on the campus located in South Central Los Angeles, between West 78th and 79th streets and between Vermont and Normandie Avenues. The college had bought the houses circling the campus to house faculty and administrators. The residents of the rest of the community were all black.

In the early 1960s there were hardly half a dozen black students, but as the decade progressed, more and more black students enrolled at Pepperdine. The residence hall students were predominately white, while the black students came from the surrounding area. Not all of the students were members of Churches of Christ, but they all knew the requirements of the college before enrolling, and attending chapel was one of them. One of my favorite scenes was to watch the students cross the campus to chapel. Some students were creative in finding reasons not to attend.

Changes were made in 1963, when Jennings Davis joined our ranks as dean of students. Since Dean Sanders had added the title "associate dean of students" to my job description, Dr. Davis and I became a team, working and praying together. Prayer sustained us as we supervised, planned, participated, disciplined and encouraged in all areas of student life—even talking with cafeteria managers when Chinese students complained that the rice was sticky.

The Holy Spirit had planted in my heart an intense love for students of all colors and sizes. This love turned the most difficult work into joy as I served them.

The civil unrest of the late 60s and early 70s filtered onto our campus. Women students were busy writing letters and mailing care packages to soldiers in Vietnam. Later, they signed petitions to Congress to end the war. Traditional college activities such as pledge week turned into campus demonstrations. As hostilities grew, Dr. Davis and I realized that there was no choice for Christian workers but to pray. We selected groups of students, paired them and scheduled them to pray night and day.

Often I was aware of the work of the Holy Spirit helping and guiding us. In one of the most discouraging times, fires were being set and graffiti appeared on the walls of the men's restroom. It appeared to be the work of black students, but our office discovered that a white student was doing it to discredit the blacks. The forces of good and evil were at work on our campus, as well as in our nation. Perceptions and distortions were working against the Spirit, and I wondered, if God were to deal with us on the issue of race, how many of us would have leprosy as Miriam did because of Moses' wife?

During these years I accepted invitations to speak at meetings of the Associated Women for Pepperdine (AWP), a fund-raising association created by Helen Young, President Young's wife. I also spoke frequently at church camps and activities for women up and down the coast, in addition to my regular duties as dean. At times a student would drive me to a speaking engagement while I rested in the back seat.

Closing Doors

I knew that the Holy Spirit, having brought me to Pepperdine to glorify Christ in all that I did, would release me when that work was finished. When the college began its move to Malibu, I found all doors closed to me for working at the new campus. As a result of this move, I "re-invented" myself. I designed a course entitled "Women in Contemporary Society" and submitted it to Jack Scott, Provost, for submission to the Academic Council. The course was approved.

Just then my mother died unexpectedly. While I was grieving for her, my father's health began to decline, so I petitioned the college to put me on half-time so I could help my brother with our father. He died the next year. I was numbed by grief, despite knowing that both were happier where they were.

As the undergraduate students completed their work and moved to the Malibu campus, the Los Angeles campus became a graduate school. There was little left for my office to do but write recommendations for students. The only door open for me professionally was to get a license in family therapy, a course that Dr. Davis also decided to pursue. Going back to school had always been rejuvenating to me. I enrolled in classes for the family therapy license, which Pepperdine University offered at the Marriage and Family Institute in Hollywood. I also served as dean to the Pepperdine students for a year, making sure they paid their tuition and got their grades in time to graduate. After completing my degree, I began to offer therapy classes. The years flew by and my classes flourished, so that after 18 years at Pepperdine, I locked my office door for the last time and moved into my new office in Torrance, California, as a therapist. Some Pepperdine friends hosted a wonderful farewell banquet in my honor.

My love for students never diminished. To this day I keep a small manila envelope with the notation "For Cheer on Bad Days." In that envelope, I found an undated, unsigned typed note which reads:

> Mrs. Todd,
>
> Pepperdine College needs you so much. You are so definitely a part of the pulse of the school. Many students look to you for wisdom and guidance. To many people inside and outside the college, you symbolize the spirit of the Christian ideals upon which Pepperdine was founded. There are many of us who are concerned that you stay here to help us....We love you—many more of us than you know.

Because of encouraging words like these, the joy of working with students remained with me as more and more of the campus personnel and undergraduate students moved to the Malibu campus.

Racism in the Church
Despite scriptures that read, "We're all one in Christ Jesus—neither male nor female, bond or free," our history in Churches of Christ abounds with stories of discrimination and segregation. If, for example, not too many years past, black persons had the temerity to attend a white congregation, a special place was reserved for them in the balcony or on the front row. This reflected our cultural heritage. It was the way everyone in our society behaved. But it made me wonder, "How is the church different from the world?"

Of course, racism is a two-way street. Seldom do we deliberately offend those of a different race. Often we just don't see them. Since we don't see them, we never get to know them. The prejudice of the world remains dormant in our hearts until a situation causes it to be expressed. The use of the terms "black church" and "white church" implies separation—missing God's blessings of mutual fellowship.

The turbulent years of the late 60s and the early 70s revealed to many the difficulty of defining racial problems within the church. Demonstrations by black people created fear in the hearts of white people—particularly on college and university campuses. My own experiences working on racial reconciliation are among my most precious memories. The activities were often painful, as emotions can be very raw and intense, but there was also the sweet, comforting and strengthening presence of God through the Spirit.

Experiences in the lives of black brothers and sisters differ from those of white brothers and sisters, leading to different perceptions. Attitudes develop which, much like genetic traits, pass from generation to generation. For example, many whites assumed it was their "right" to have black servants and not treat black people as equals. Intervention had to take place before changes could be made; for instance, the first time a black man told a white man, "Don't call me boy." The era and culture in which we live usually determine how that intervention will be received or acted upon. I personally experienced ways that intervention and reconciliation can occur between the races.

In an all-white town in central Texas around 1963, a young black student rode with my husband and me to my parents' home. The young woman's fiancé met us there. The next day was Sunday, and I pulled my father aside and asked him to make sure there was no scene over the black couple's presence in the church building. He asked the young man to sit with him at the front of the building, and the young lady sat between my mother and me. As the service began, my father asked the young man, "Brother Smith, please lead us in prayer." As a result, the congregation was friendly to the young couple; and there was no scene except God being glorified. My parents both accepted and practiced equality among brothers and sisters in Christ.

A year or so later my parents were visiting my home in California as we concluded our weekly prayer meeting of male and female students. With tears in his eyes and a voice trembling with emotion, an elderly gospel preacher said, "This is the first time I have ever heard women pray. The fervency and love for God in their voices is over-whelming and beautiful to hear." One by one the students passed the elderly man, taking his hand and that of his wife. Not a word was said. None was needed. Later, as the train pulled away from the station on their way home, my father raised his hand as if in benediction and said, "Hang in there, Deborah," an allusion to the Old Testament judge.

Discrimination because of skin color was reflected in all areas of American life, affecting jobs, income, promotions and respect. The Civil Rights movement created tensions even among Christians of the same race. A similar phenomenon occurred in the women's move-ment. The women's movement began as a protest against inequality in the workplace over equal pay for equal work. Over a hundred years earlier, women who were active in the anti-slavery movement began to see parallels with their own legal, economic and social standing. They lobbied for the right to vote and for economic independence.

In the 1960s women again saw parallels between their own status and that of blacks. When we began to see young Christian students being affected by these hostilities, my friend Ruby Holland and I felt the Holy Spirit moving us. Ruby suggested that we get an interracial group of women together to encourage communication. She repre-sented the black community and I the white. We invited the officers of two Christian education groups, one black and one white, to an over-night retreat out of the city. We prayed and planned, and our friends began to join us.

Our evening program began with prayer and a meal prepared by the president of the white group. Each white woman had a black part-ner to get acquainted with during the meal. After dinner a black col-lege professor addressed the group on race in our society. Then she showed a film about a white minister in a northern state trying to inte-grate his white congregation with a black congregation.

Following the presentation and a period of relaxation, the dinner partners were formed into groups of ten. Trained Christian leaders led group discussions. Each had a list of pertinent questions, and the women explained how they thought and felt. When negative feelings surfaced, the leaders kept the women working until understanding was reached. The group work was followed by an assembly for singing, scripture reading and prayer, and the women told each other goodnight.

While others slept, Ruby, Ruth Bales and I critiqued the day's events. We felt the effort was worthwhile and should be continued.

The next morning at breakfast, the partners ate together and visited. Following a general assembly for prayer and scripture reading, the groups formed again to discuss the material they heard the night before. The assembly was called to order, and with reverence and joy, we praised God for the experiences of the weekend. It was nearing noontime, the scheduled time for closure, but the women were unwilling to leave. We sang hymns of praise to our Lord for two hours, parting with assurance that we would meet again soon.

Within a few days, Ruby, her friend Elsie Meeks, Ruth Bales and I met to draw up bylaws and a constitution for our nonprofit organization, "The Center for Women's Studies." Our husbands provided a house for our headquarters, and we began to recruit "founding members." The first order of business was to plan and send out notices of our next meeting, a potluck luncheon on the patio of our recently obtained house. New people joined us, and we began to meet in each other's homes for potlucks and programs, praise and prayer.

Group members began visiting various congregations. We would contact an elder or the minister and ask if we could visit. Many of the congregations we visited served us lunch after worship, and during lunch one of us would "tell our story."

We developed a cadre of speakers who spoke at seminars, ladies' days, Bible classes and lectureships. During the early 70s, four of our members gave a presentation at the National Conference of Collegiate Women Deans in Detroit.

In the early years we included a youth group in our annual retreat and subsidized their fees. We believed that teenage women needed to be involved in interracial, spiritual programs. We established a newsletter and recommended books for reading. At some of the early meetings, women from the group reviewed *The Biography of Sojourner Truth* and *Black Like Me,* and in the 1990s, *The Color of Water.*

During our annual retreat, which extends from Friday afternoon through noon Sunday, we invite local ministers to preach for us, and my husband is usually in charge of the communion. Ours is a spiritual retreat. Members and invited speakers focus on the theme for the weekend.

In the late 70s the house was sold, and we stopped offering classes for the community. Instead, we used our homes to plan and work. Our energies became more focused on our annual retreat. For the past three years, two congregations have sent monetary gifts to provide scholarships for the youth. Other than occasional fund-raisers, we have no operational funds. We try to keep expenses down, particularly hotel costs, so everyone can attend.

After all these years as a group, we have stories we remind each other of often. Some are sad, some are gentle and some are humorous. Some of our sisters have already gone to be with Jesus; the rest of us are much older than when we began. College students have become grandmothers and middle-aged women, elderly. Skin colors and differences in beliefs have vanished. Now we are truly sisters in faith.

As the black community rises into the middle class, some are buying homes in white neighborhoods; in some congregations of white people, black faces can be seen. In society at large this change contrasts with the population movement in the 1960s and 70s when whites moved away as blacks moved in. Still, there are strong pockets of racism in our society. In contrast, it is good to know that there are pockets of love, communion and fellowship in Christ. Our group "passed the color line" years ago, and we have been blessed by God in our ministry of reconciliation.

To work with women who were formed in their Christian walk by oppression in our society, as well as in the liberty of our Savior, is to enter a new dimension of compassion and love. Worship through song is as necessary to the women as food. As we meet for potluck lunches there is always time for singing hymns. Black women taught us their songs and we taught them ours. The common denominator is our faith and love in the Lord. The Apostle Paul wrote the Ephesian church that "There is one body and one Spirit—just as you were called to one hope, one baptism; one God and Father of all, who is over all and through all and in all" (Eph. 4:4-5).

The first meeting of our annual retreat, on Friday evening, we have a time of quiet, and each person writes out her sins on a card. Then each one takes the card to the front of the room and puts it in a basket or hangs it on a wooden cross. The leader for this exercise prays over the cards, asking God for forgiveness. Then the cards are torn up and put into a waste basket, symbolizing the Savior's grace.

In recent years our emphasis shifted from black and white to include all the ethnic groups around us. Women of other races and cultures, usually friends of regular attendees, come to be with us. On a small scale, multi-ethnicity is a reality. God is willing to help us learn to love and care for each other. And the Spirit will bless other groups that come together from different races and cultures to share in worship and joy as God's children. If we learn to set aside our beliefs about each other and about how God works, we will experience first-hand the blessings of sisterhood in Christ.

Lucille Todd graduated from Trinity University and holds the M.A. from St. Mary's University, both in San Antonio, Texas. She earned her Ph.D. in social psychology from International College in Los Angeles with a doctoral thesis on "Myth, Symbol, and Interracial Understanding." She also holds a Certificate in Black Studies from UCLA.

A teacher, lecturer, former Dean of Women at Pepperdine and retired psychotherapist, Lucile is also a wife, mother, grandmother and great-grandmother. She and her husband Bill live in Fort Worth, Texas. They have two children.

18

A Balanced Life?

Jeanine Varner

"Anything worth doing is worth overdoing." That was my family's motto as I was growing up, a motto which shaped my childhood and even my adult life.

My friends and my siblings' friends know our family motto and joke about it with us. They understand that it applied to everything we did as kids—well, to everything that was "worth doing." And what was "worth doing"? Almost anything—scrubbing the kitchen floor, studying for a history exam, learning to play a musical instrument, eating corn on the cob, playing Scrabble, the list goes on and on. They understand, too, that it still applies to what we do and who we are as adults.

The motto is a bit of a joke. It acknowledges its own excess. But as kids we knew it wasn't really a laughing matter. We knew that we were to work hard—very hard—at whatever we did. In fact, that motto and all it represents may be our parents' greatest legacy to us. They didn't have a lot of money. They didn't have a college education. But they gave us a great blessing: an awareness of the joy of whole-hearted work, hard-headed commitment to whatever task was at hand.

You may suspect that ours wasn't a well-balanced life, and your suspicion may be correct. But I want to suggest that "balance" may be an over-rated virtue and, at times, perhaps, not a virtue at all.

Christian women often speak of the virtue of balance. They tell of their efforts to balance their personal life and their professional life, their time with children and their time with their spouse, their work at church and their work at home, their labor and their leisure. The image that comes to my mind when I hear a woman speak of balance is the image of a trained seal, balancing a brightly colored beach ball on her nose and barking gleefully after completing her performance. The performance may be clever and charming, but it accomplishes nothing. It is pointless.

Is Balance a Virtue?

Is balance really a virtue?

Aristotle, the father of ancient Greek philosophy, believed it was. Aristotle described virtues as "means between extremes." He explained that courage, for example, is the mean between cowardice on the one hand and rashness on the other. Similarly, he saw liberality as the mean between wastefulness on the one hand and stinginess on the other. Aristotle believed that reason would lead man (not woman, of course, in Aristotle's day) to choose the mean between the extremes and would thus lead him toward a virtuous life.

Aristotle's rational approach to virtue is rather appealing. It's balanced and orderly. It has stood the test of time. Even today we speak of Aristotle's "golden mean." But Aristotle's "golden mean" is fundamentally opposed to Christianity—which is passionate, extravagant radical. Even irrational.

What is rational about the incarnation? Why would the almighty God come into our world as a helpless infant? From his birth, as Isaiah's messianic prophecy tells us, "he had no beauty or majesty to attract us to him, nothing in his appearance that we should desire him." Throughout his life, "he was despised and rejected by men, a man of sorrows, and familiar with suffering." Why would he come to us "like one from whom men hide their faces," so that he "was despised, and we esteemed him not"? The incarnation defies reason!

What is rational about the crucifixion? Why would almighty God take the form of a suffering servant? Why would the Word take the form of a dumb sheep, silent before its slaughterers? Why would God allow his Son to be smitten, afflicted, "pierced for our transgressions," "crushed for our iniquities"? Why did our Savior, the life-bringer, lose his life on the cross? The crucifixion defies reason!

What is rational about the resurrection? How could the one who "was assigned a grave with the wicked" live again? "After the suffering of his soul," how could the one who was buried rise again to "see the light of life"? How could that Light, once extinguished, triumph over darkness? The resurrection defies reason!

The God who gave us the ability to reason demands an extravagant, passionate, radical faith—faith in an infant Messiah, a suffering Servant, a risen Lord. He demands a response which is total, undivided, unbalanced—a response based not on reason but on faith.

Jesus Demands a Total Response

He demands a response like that of Paul. When the persecutor came to see the truth on the road to Damascus, his response had to be passionate. He had to go into the very temples where he had persecuted Christians and live as a radical Christian! He could not simply seek a reasonable mean between the extremes. He had to be the extreme, the follower of Jesus, the disciple for whom "to live is Christ" and "to die is gain"!

He demands a response like that of the poor widow who gave her two coins. Her response to Jesus had to be extravagant. Unlike the rich people, who threw large amounts of money into the temple treasury, she gave all she had, her last coins, extravagantly, unreasonably. Jesus acknowledged that response, saying to his disciples, "I tell you the truth, this poor widow has put more into the treasury than all the others. They all gave out of their wealth; but she, out of her poverty, put in everything—all she had to live on."

He demands a response like that of the woman who gave her perfume to her Savior. Her response to Jesus was radical, embarrassingly extreme, you may say. She brought an alabaster jar of perfume, wet Jesus' feet with her tears, kissed his feet, and poured perfume on them! Her radical, passionate response to her Savior was hardly balanced.

And yet her Lord praised her for her extravagant love, saying to Simon, "Do you see this woman? I came into your house. You did not give me any water for my feet, but she wet my feet with her tears and wiped them with her hair. You did not give me a kiss, but this woman, from the time I entered, has not stopped kissing my feet. Therefore, I tell you, her many sins have been forgiven—for she loved much."

I want to be that woman! Unreasonable! Unbalanced!

I want to be a woman who is radical, extravagant and passionate about the things that matter. If they are truly worth doing, they are worth overdoing.

Unfortunately, I may often choose instead to pursue a "balanced" life. I may try to balance my family life, my professional life, my spiritual life. I may try to live my life as if I'm constructing a balanced meal—a moderately proportioned serving from each major food group.

But living a life isn't really like planning a meal. A life lived fully may have no balance at all.

If I am a wife, can I really establish boundaries concerning my husband? Can I love him reasonably, moderately, proportionately?

If I am a mother, can I love my children in a balanced way? Can I decide what boundaries are reasonable, making sure that each one has an appropriate amount of my time, my effort, my love—neither more nor less than the other?

Can I decide what is a reasonable amount of time to spend on my professional life? If I believe I am called by God to use my talents in his service, can I decide exactly how much I should give? Can I decide that one talent is his, to be used in his service? Oh, God, what if the Master expected me to use five talents, totally, completely in his service?

Can I determine a reasonable way to live my spiritual life? What separates my spiritual life from my professional life or from my family life? Where are the boundaries? Where does one life begin and the other end?

In the pursuit of a merely balanced life, I may eliminate the possibility of the passionate life, the extravagant life, the radical life God wishes for me—a life totally, completely committed to him.

Seeing No Boundaries

I remember vividly an incident which occurred in a Bible class I attended at my congregation when I was a sophomore in college. The teacher asked the students, all college age women, what we wanted to do with our lives after we graduated—what we wanted to be when we grew up, so to speak. Eagerly, I responded that I wanted to be a college English professor, as I believed that God had given me the talents to do so. Others responded eagerly too, describing their hopes and plans for their futures. And then I remember the teacher's response. She said, with a sigh of great disappointment, that she was sorry that not one of us had said we wanted to be a wife and a mother. And I remember my own disappointment in turn. Had I been too eager to tell of my hopes and plans? Had I been too sure of my talents? Should I have said, "Lord willing"? Should I have said, "In my spare time"? Should I have said, "As part of a balanced life"?

Over the years I have come to realize that the problem was hers, not mine. She saw boundaries. Family life, to her, was not professional life. Professional life, to her, was not spiritual life. I have come to see otherwise. I believe that my life is a whole. No boundaries. When I am teaching my students well, I am serving God. When I am serving God, I am being a good mother, showing my daughter and my son how to use their talents. When I am being a good mother, I am teaching my students. When I fail, I fail as a person—not as a wife, a mother, a teacher, a Christian. No boundaries.

My best teachers have been those who saw no boundaries. They are the ones who did not have professional lives, or family lives, or spiritual lives. They simply lived their whole lives in God's service, and they inspired me to try to do so as well. From the first day of my freshman year at Oklahoma Christian University, Bailey McBride was such a person. Bailey was then, and remains today, a marvelous teacher, one who has inspired thousands of students during more than three decades of teaching. His students have always known that when they witnessed him explicating a poem, critiquing a research paper, mentoring a student, or nurturing his own children and grandchildren, they were seeing a whole person. The same person. A man of God using the many talents with which he has been abundantly blessed.

Bailey has been my mentor for more than thirty years now. When I was a freshman he showed me that he trusted me to be at once a serious student and a committed Christian. He never made me think I ought to balance the two. Throughout undergraduate school and graduate school, he showed me that he trusted me to become a capable college teacher. He never made me wonder if I could or should balance my academic life and my spiritual life. He knew there should be no boundaries, and he made me know it as well. When I was a young wife and mother and teacher, he took for granted that I could and would use the talents God had given me. He made me confident enough not to put boundaries around them or to bury them for safe-keeping until a later day.

The Demands of the Light

When I was asked five years ago to serve as Vice President of Academic Affairs at Oklahoma Christian University, Bailey gave me the confidence to take on what seemed then—and remains—a daunting challenge. He knew what a challenge it was; he had held that position for more than twenty years himself. He knew how daunting it would be to try to lead the faculty and academic programs of a rapidly growing and changing university. He had mentored me since my teenage years, and he knew my many weaknesses and limitations. But he trusted me nevertheless. His confidence in me as a whole person gave me confidence to be a whole person and to use as fully as possible the talents with which God has blessed me.

As a mentor, Bailey trusted me to use my talents. I pray that I can in some way merit that trust. I don't pray for balance. I pray that I can trust God enough to be extravagant, passionate, even unreasonable in serving him with everything he has given me.

Aristotle's "golden mean" may seem appealing, even virtuous. But Aristotle's teacher, Plato, knew better than his student. Plato understood that Truth demanded not moderation but passion. In his Allegory of the Cave, Plato described a group of prisoners who lived their lives in an underground cave, illuminated only indirectly by a fire which cast shadows on the cave walls. Accustomed to their world of darkness, the prisoners believed that the shadows they saw on the walls of the cave were the real thing. When one prisoner broke free of his chains and caught a glimpse of the world above, however, he risked everything to return to the cave and tell his fellow prisoners. Whatever the cost, they had to see the world which is true and real.

Living four centuries before Christ, in ancient Greece, Plato did not know the Light of the World, but he understood that the light of the world outside the cave demanded a radical response from the prisoners, who had known only the shadows. How much more does that Light demand of me?

Should my response to the Light be reasonable, a mean between extremes? My prayer is not for a balanced life. My prayer is for a whole life—a passionate, extravagant, trusting life. Because anything worth doing is worth overdoing.

Jeanine Varner is vice president of academic affairs at Oklahoma Christian University. She and her husband Paul have two children.

Jeanine holds the B.A. from Oklahoma Christian, the M.A. and Ph.D. from the University of Tennessee.

She serves on the Institutional Actions Council of the North Central Association and in the Executive Leadership Development Institute Mentoring Program of the Council of Christian Colleges and Universities. She has served as chair of the National Conference of Academic Deans. She received the Alumnus of the Year-Service to the University Award and was named to the Gaylord Chair of Distinguished Teaching at Oklahoma Christian.

19

'A Little Step Along the Way'

Karen Logan

"Mo-ses! Mo-ses!" my five-year-old lungs bellowed across the front yard. I held out a "rod" as my playmates and I re-enacted scenes from Cecile B. De Mille's epic movie, *The Ten Commandments*. At the time my family lived in Bangkok, Thailand, where my father taught for two years as an advisor to the Technical Institutes. We were there when the first missionaries from Churches of Christ arrived in 1954.

I was acting, or perhaps more accurately, acting out, at an early age. While other girls dreamed of growing up to be teachers or nurses, I longed to cross the stage and accept an Oscar. So, I've always been a little out of touch with reality. Or have I?

In the fourth grade my teacher suggested I play the role of Pandora in the sixth graders' PTA production. My mother made a pink chiffon costume. It was heavenly. Backstage the sixth graders asked me, "Aren't you nervous?" I was not. In the sixth grade, I had one line in the junior high musical Tom Sawyer. "We'd better be going, it's getting late." It was an important line. Those who did not follow my exit got lost in the cave.

When I was two, my dad asked me to sing "Daniel in the Lion's Den" in front of his relatives. I was the first grandchild. "You Ain't Nothin' But a Hound Dog," was the lyric that escaped from my innocent lips. My grandmother saved me from a spanking.

Religious training was the best part of my upbringing. Mom and Dad lived what they taught. We had family devotions and memorized scripture together. They constantly helped people, took people to church and showed filmstrip Bible studies. My parents blessed me with acceptance and praise.

Besides the two years overseas, my early years were spent in the northern United States. When I was a toddler, my parents drove 60 miles one way to church, making a regular stop due to my motion sickness. In Michigan Mother taught one class for all the kids in a small congregation. She had no curriculum. She bought each student a brown spiral notebook, and we copied Bible verses and glued pictures into it. When we moved away from Pennsylvania, my Sunday school teacher gave me a bracelet. I still have it. I will admit, also, to the time Julie and I discovered where the leftover unleavened bread was tossed after the evening service, and we scurried out at the final amen to sneak a bite.

At ten I began to consider being baptized. My father baptized me in an old one-room schoolhouse-type church building in Michigan.

When we moved to Tennessee, I had the opportunity to attend Christian schools. My parents later told me that they chose a congregation for worship where they thought my sister and I would have friends. Now that I have raised children, I know what that kind of decision means. Dad became an elder at the age of 35 and has served two different congregations of the Lord's church in that capacity for nearly 35 years. My mother teaches toddlers and adult women and coordinates senior activities and the annual ladies' day.

Two things stand out as faith-shaping events during my high school years. My dad loved to travel and we had the most marvelous family vacations. On one trip we visited Eureka Springs, Arkansas, and saw the outdoor production of the Passion Play, the last week of the life of Christ. Thirty-three years ago, it was a novelty. Hundreds of audience members sat in a hillside stadium and watched the play below as if watching a movie being filmed. The voices were taped and broadcast over large speakers as the actors pantomimed their parts. The sun set, and the trial of Jesus took place at dusk. He was crucified on a small hill to the side of the stadium. The most memorable scene was when Jesus suddenly appeared in the upper room after his resurrection.

For years, whenever I took communion, I tearfully recalled the Passion Play and the reality of Christ's life and death. That experience brought the Bible to life for me. Recently, I mentioned to my sister the influence that play had on my life, and she agreed. She wanted to take her family there, because it had inspired her as well.

The second influential event occurred when a guest preacher held a meeting at our congregation and met with several families in our home. The visiting minister showed us how to sit in a circle, hold hands, take turns praying aloud, and squeeze the hand next to us when we finished praying so they would know when to begin their prayer. Even the women and teenagers prayed. Today everyone knows what a chain prayer is, but that was the first time I had experienced one, and it seemed rather daring at the time. I was excited! Chain prayers gave religion spontaneity and emotion outside of the pew, and I could actively participate.

Maybe it was exciting because it was dangerous. Even as a teenager I knew what women were allowed to do and not do in public worship. To pray aloud with a group of adults was a thrill. It was invigorating to speak to God in a more personal way with other Christians. But years later some have questioned my motives. "Why do you want to pray in front of the congregation?" The question deserves an honest answer.

How does a woman know why she wants to lead a prayer or offer communion devotions or teach adult classes? The same way a man knows? Is it for personal recognition? Is it to push the envelope, because I know that I would not be allowed to do it in most Churches of Christ? If you asked a Christian man why he volunteered to lead a prayer or teach a class, his answer might be that God has given him the ability, that he wants to share the good news with others, that he grows spiritually from the experience, that he has some devotional ideas to relate to the Christian life. Why can't a woman have the same motivation?

In high school my calling to participate in church work led me to help my mother teach her Sunday school class of kindergartners. They were too young for me, and I graduated to become the third grade teacher's assistant. These students could read and do what you asked them to do. I thought I had found my niche, but at school I still floundered, searching for what I could do best. I tried out for cheerleader, tennis, basketball and chorus. We didn't have a band. Without fail, I made the first cut, but never the final team. Later, I reasoned that it was due to my acting ability. I knew enough about a lot of things to act like I knew what I was doing. But my expertise was in the acting, not the skills needed for the activity.

During my junior and senior years, God flung open some doors for me. I was elected to serve as an officer of various clubs—secretary of Civinettes, president of the Pep Club and the Thespians. My junior year, I was an understudy for the class play. During my senior year, a teacher initiated the speech and drama club, and I finally had an outlet for my "acting out." I performed a dramatic interpretation from Macbeth for our school talent show and tied for first place. At home after the talent show, my dad casually commented on the high unemployment rate among actors!

This was at a Christian high school, so I had numerous opportunities to learn the Bible as well as participate in benevolent service. I memorized scripture, sang at the nursing home, suggested a sermon topic to our minister, and was active in our youth classes at church. Being chosen by my teachers as the female recipient of the "I Dare You Award" gave me confidence in my leadership ability.

At a Christian college, I continued to be involved in theater activities during my freshman and sophomore years. Then God guided me into more leadership opportunities. I served as president of our girls' social club, devotional leader for the newly formed Women's Student Representative Organization, and girls' leader for our summer campaign group. My roommate and I audited a Greek class, and Bible courses were easy and enjoyable for me. Lessons from knowledgeable Bible scholars and a minister who was not afraid to question tradition encouraged me to do the same.

Still unsure of what career to pursue, each semester I changed my major. Before starting college I had considered speech, but I didn't want to teach and was uninformed as to what could be done with a speech degree. Home economics seemed a wise choice since I was not very gifted in homemaking. After all, the bottom line was to get married and raise a Christian family. Here again, hindsight has revealed some unspoken guidelines. The parents of the Baby Boom generation worked hard so their daughters could get an education. These women were expected to take advantage of parental sacrifice. They were expected to go to college and...? Get married? So it seemed logical to me to study something practical. However, my first home economics course was so difficult, I thought I'd never make it. After wandering back to speech classes, which I excelled in, for a semester, I finally landed in social work. I wanted to work with people. My senior year I helped plan the first social work seminar and lived off campus doing my field placement.

Meantime, for three summers I had gone on mission campaigns in the northeastern United States. A male and a female were usually paired for door-knocking and conducting Bible studies. If a woman or a teenage girl was interested in a Bible study, we girls could teach them. And of course, we got to do half the talking at the doors. I loved this work. Each year campaigners had to raise money for their summer trip as well as for school in the fall. I wrote numerous letters, telephoned preachers and elders, and set up speaking appointments for the male students to speak at various congregations in my hometown to raise money for our campaigns. One year the adult campaign treasurer commented on our meeting, "Oh, you're the one who raised all that money!" Traveling, teaching the Bible and meeting new people were rewarding and fulfilling to me.

Having no marriage prospects at graduation, I moved not far from home and began a short-lived social work career. I was miserable. One pleasant aspect of the job was working with foster children. In case I ever did get married, teaching elementary children appeared to be an ideal job. I could be home with my children when they were home. Ironic, since I neither wanted to be a teacher nor had homemaking skills, but I believed this was my ultimate goal—to raise a Christian family. Hoping that a teacher's schedule and routine would better suit my personality, I decided to volunteer for a third grade class and make a trial run.

The classroom setting did provide more structure, yet it allowed for creativity that was missing in social work. The Lord gave the go-ahead for an elementary teaching degree. While working on this certification, I dated a wonderful Christian man from our singles group at church and proposed to him! Then he agreed to propose to me. My father performed our ceremony just as he had done for my sister's wedding five months earlier. My parents' backyard was the setting for our wedding, and I wanted my mother and father to walk me down the aisle to "give me away." Years later I recognized this as an egalitarian tendency, but at the time I just knew I loved both parents and wanted to honor them both for their sacrifice and love in raising me.

Dad: Who gives this woman to be married?

Mom: Her father and I.

My mother preferred not to be honored in this way!

Following two years of teaching third grade in a Christian school, our first boy was born. We named him after my dad and Batsell Barrett Baxter. Two years later to the day, our second boy was named after two New Testament apostles. Since high school, I had wanted to name a baby girl Keturah, after Abraham's second wife. My husband was relieved when we had two sons. Our verbal pre-nuptial agreement (we didn't call it that then) stated that a stay-at-home Mom was best, and raising my kids was one of the greatest joys of my life. I could teach and play at the same time!

As the younger child entered school, I went back to teaching—for two weeks. Stress from several different directions made "the perfect job" unbearable. A Christian counselor, Prozac, daily calls from my mother and close friends were what the Lord provided for me at this time in my life.

A home party saleswoman, a Mother's Morning Out teacher, and a children's Sunday school teacher were other roles I tried to plug into. I prayed God to show me how I could best serve him. Considering my abilities and education, it seemed I should do something great for the Lord. Bored at home, I searched for a new career. After a variety of interviews and a stint for a temporary employment agency, I quit searching, but I kept praying, "God, what do you want me to do?"

During this confusing stage of my life, God provided a new friend at church. She and I threw ourselves into the children's education program. We traveled to a large congregation to observe their children's department and brought ideas back home. Having had experience conducting teacher training workshops, my friend trained me and a third woman, and the education minister asked us to hold a workshop. I was apprehensive about appearing more knowledgeable than I really was, but I was assured that many teachers actually wanted to be trained. There was a great deal of interest and excitement about the techniques that were new then: learning centers, team teaching, painting murals in church hallways, audio-visual equipment, writing curriculum, puppets, drama and designing your own Vacation Bible School. The three of us made a good team, and I found the work fulfilling.

We began writing our own VBS material, and I organized the drama skits and coordinated VBS for two years. As our education minister was resigning, he recommended me to head children's education. Knowledge of the congregation, administrative and organizational skills, and the ability to work with all ages were my credentials. The elders offered me a part-time job directing the Mother's Morning Out program for preschoolers and directing the children's education program for our 400-member congregation. It seemed to me that one part-time job plus one part-time job did not equal one part-time job. They would not offer it to a man on a part-time salary. They accepted my counter offer of one part-time job as children's education director. My husband jokingly referred to me as a "Ministerette."

This was in 1990, and as I began attending professional meetings, I learned that women in Churches of Christ were serving (paid and unpaid) in limited locales as children's education coordinators, counselors, worship planners and benevolence ministers.

Blessed to be at a progressive church, I was included in the ministers' luncheons (at my request) and my picture was included with the three other ministers (at their request) in our local newspaper ad. This was disturbing to some other congregations. Our music minister asked me to participate with the other ministers and read a poem at our Wednesday night July fourth devotion, which occurred in the fellowship hall, not the auditorium, due to a smaller crowd and the informality of the service. This was a first-time occurrence and although no one said anything negative to me, there were complaints about a woman reading publicly.

One of my last official duties was to execute a teachers' appreciation dinner. Having seen a musical skit performed at a workshop, I recruited actors and asked the music minister to sing for this inspiring program in praise of Sunday school teachers. After I emceed the dinner and performed in the skit, a mature male member looked me in the eye and said, "We need to use you in a more public way."

Soon my family and I left that congregation for our children to have the advantage of a mature youth program, even though our new congregation was much more traditional. They did, however, have a part-time woman on staff who was their children's education minister, and she included me in her ministry. I coordinated and performed the same teachers' skit for this congregation's teachers' appreciation dinner and again for a banquet honoring the teenagers' favorite public and private school teachers. Recruiting for and directing the VBS dramas was my project for a couple of years.

Continuing to attend professional conferences, I enjoyed the worship of hand-raising and singing; on one occasion an elder Christian brother beside me remarked, "I can see God has made you to express your emotions outwardly in worship. Do not stifle this gift." Tears came to my eyes, I excused myself and wept privately. My current home congregation did not accept such outward expressions. How could I use what God had given me? "God," I sobbed, "what do you want me to do?"

My girlfriend and I wanted to be involved with our kids, so we volunteered as chaperones for the youth group and traveled to the Harding University campus. While there we decided to take advantage of the library.

For some time, we had been asking ourselves questions:

"Where is the verse that says a woman cannot teach a boy after he is baptized?"

"Where is the verse that says a woman cannot lead a prayer?"

"Where is the verse that says a mother cannot baptize her child?"

"Where is the verse that says a woman can start a song from the pew but cannot stand in front and lead a song?"

"Why can a woman greet visitors and hand out bulletins in the foyer but not usher the same visitors to a seat in the auditorium?"

I still get teary-eyed every time I sit in a pew and watch a newly baptized, 10-year-old boy read a scripture and wonder why a mature, 40-year-old Christian woman cannot. One of our friends said she did not care to join us in our search for answers, because she anticipated the friction it might cause.

We spent hours in the library searching for brotherhood articles, tapes and books. As we stretched out in a dorm room, poring over our copied materials, my friend asked me to read one article out loud and explain it. "You can understand that stuff easier than I can," she said. After a pause, her eyes grew wide and she asked me, "If you had been born a male, would you have become a preacher?" I told her my mom had jokingly called me "preacher" while I was growing up, but I think it was due to my forthright and argumentative nature. Nevertheless, I considered it a compliment. Occasionally, others have referred to me as "preacher." One woman told me she dreamed that I led a prayer at church.

Our study led us on an eye-opening journey, which included cassette tapes from Pepperdine lectures, a book of Freed-Hardeman lectures, and articles from the *Gospel Advocate* written by David Lipscomb in the 1880's and 1890's. An Abilene professor had just edited a volume of essays and was soon to publish another. We read evangelical books with opposing views on women's role in the church. We learned what hierarchalists, traditionalists, complimentarians and egalitarians were. We even discovered there were Biblical feminists! Some facts made our heads spin, while others caused our hearts to soar.

Several women inspired us. Mrs. T. P. (Selena Moore) Holman wrote several letters in 1888 to the *Gospel Advocate* about the inconsistencies of the church's interpretation of women's roles. Clara Babcock reported to the Christian Standard newspaper in 1892 that she was an evangelist and had baptized over 300. One hundred years later, Micki Pulley's story in a 1987 issue of *Mission* magazine described her journey to a Boston church pulpit. Her sister Kathy had chosen to teach religion at a state university.

In our hunger for answers, we continually prayed that God would lead us to truth and keep us from Satan's deceptions. What we received was a blessing. Digging through piles of books and papers, we slowly unearthed a spiritual freedom that gave us a peace that we, as Christian women, had not experienced before. One of our most exciting discoveries was a two-page advertisement in a 1990 issue of *Christianity Today.* A statement of faith by Christians for Biblical Equality, it opened, "The Bible teaches the full equality of men and women in Creation and in Redemption (Genesis 1:26-28, 2:23, 5:1-2; 1 Corinthians 11:11-12; Galatians 3:13, 28, 5:1)."

Eager to share our life-changing information, we compiled a bibliography and submitted an outline for 13 lessons of adult study on "Women's Role in the Church." Naively, we hoped to teach the class. The education minister said he had never seen such thorough research. He and an elder conducted the class in the auditorium on Wednesday nights. Our materials were not well utilized. There was little discussion as the setting was not suited for it, and although the education minister tried to present some different ideas to consider, the elder just confirmed the traditions of Churches of Christ. "Study" over. Case closed.

Due to our research, however, I was offered a part-time job as a research assistant by the adult education minister. I was paid by the hour and had a sympathetic boss who continually apologized for not being able to put my name with his on the materials we were writing. While working for him, I was taking graduate Bible courses, thinking I might like to teach college or high school Bible courses. After talking with several administrators, it was clear that our fellowship would only allow me to teach females, even in a school setting. Although I dropped out of the program, I was encouraged by a remark made by a former college roommate. As she had done graduate Bible work and was employed as a campus minister, female students asked her how they could prepare for a job like hers. She informed them of the limited opportunities, but encouraged them to get a professional degree so that, if and when the door opened, they would be prepared with the same educational credentials as the men. We shared some of our "women's role" research and vowed to stay in touch. At home my friend and I began to use our materials in private studies with interested women.

As my children were now old enough for me to be out in the evenings, I turned to acting again. After ten auditions for roles in community chorus and theater productions, I landed a role as Mrs. Cratchitt in A Christmas Carol. Over the next eight years, I acted in such shows as *Harvey, Steel Magnolias, Beauty and the Beast, The Philadelphia Story, To Kill a Mockingbird, Sound of Music,* and *Grace and Glorie.* Our arts community recognizes outstanding performances each year, and I received two nominations. Meanwhile, I continued writing and directing short programs at church.

In the back of my mind, I had always thought it would be a good idea to act out Bible characters to teach a lesson, even to adults. When I was asked to lead the ladies' class in a study of the gospel of Mark, I decided it was time to begin. What better way to introduce the book than to dress up like Mary, the mother of Mark, and brag on my son? An Israeli neighbor taught me to say a few things in Hebrew and some women in the class who did not know me thought I really was from a foreign country. Later, when the congregation as a whole prepared to study Mark's gospel, I volunteered to present a brief version of "Mary, the mother of Mark," to our adult Bible teachers when we hosted a workshop for them. Our guest workshop speaker remarked that he wished I would follow him around when he teaches Mark back at his home church. I traveled to Kentucky and presented "Mary, the mother of Mark" to a senior citizens' church group (men and women) that met on Tuesdays and a Wednesday night ladies' class.

To this day, there are still men who greet me with a grin and, "How is Mary, the mother of Mark?"

A few months later a friend that I had not communicated with in several years called me and said God had put me on her heart. She was now worshipping with a Baptist church and wanted to know if I would speak at their ladies' Christmas celebration. She did not know of my drama ventures. My presentation was "The Three Wise Women." Following dramatic reenactments of Mary, Elizabeth and Anna, we discussed how these women announced Jesus to their world and how we, in our own different ways, announce Jesus to our world. Weeks later I ran into a woman from that meeting who remembered who the three wise women were.

When I was asked at my home church to organize the ladies' Bible class schedule for the coming year, I asked, "Does this mean I can ask myself to teach?"

"Absolutely!" was the reply.

The fall curriculum would be "Women of the Bible" and would include some dramatic interpretations. Leading off with "The Three Wise Women," the series included well-known characters such as Eve and Ruth, as well as less familiar ones, Jehosheba and Joanna. The last character I portrayed was Selena Moore Holman (1850-1915), a restoration era woman from Churches of Christ who served as president of the Tennessee Christian Women's Temperance Union and wrote articles in the *Gospel Advocate* in favor of the new woman role model for motherhood. This popular lesson included information on other women of the era who served as preachers and exhorters in restoration churches. I have recently repeated this series for a Wednesday night ladies' class. There are eight different characters, including a generic Bible mother, whom I use to introduce the concluding lesson, "How Is God Like a Mother?"

After 30 years of searching, I believe God was preparing me to teach gender equality using this ministry of drama. My personality, passion and spiritual gifts have found a "stage." With confidence I am assembling actors for the first adult drama to be presented in the auditorium on a Sunday evening. I continue to research and teach and act.

In *To Kill A Mockingbird*, my character realized that racial prejudice would not be eradicated in the course of one single court case. But, "maybe," Miss Maudie hopes, "we're taking a little step ... a little step along the way." As I observe Churches of Christ in America, I see that we are taking small steps and I pray, not so patiently at times, for these steps, steps down the path to freedom for all—Jew and Gentile, slave and free, male and female, for we all are one in Christ (Gal. 3:28).

Suggested References

Allen, C. Leonard. (1993). *Distant Voices: Discovering a Forgotten Past for a Changing Church.* Abilene, TX: ACU Press.

Bristow, J. (1986). *What Paul Really Said about Women.* San Francisco: Harper.

Howard, O. (1992). "No Longer Male and Female," Pepperdine Univeristy Lecture cassettes.

Keener, C. (1992). *Paul, Women, and Wives.* Peabody, MA: Hendrickson.

Osburn, Carroll. (1993). "Women in the New Testament Church, part 1, 2, 3," Pepperdine University Lecture cassettes.

Osburn, Carroll. (ed.) (1993, 1995). *Essays on Women in Earliest Christianity (Vols. 1-2).* Joplin, MO: College Press.

Smith, Paul R. (1993). *Is It Okay To Call God "Mother:" Considering the Feminine Face of God.* Peabody, MA: Hendrickson.

Karen Olree Logan is a member of the Mayfair Church of Christ in Huntsville, Alabama, where she and her husband Granville serve as leaders of the Encouragers Class. They have two college-aged sons.

A graduate of Harding University, she has been a social worker, teacher and full-time mother. As a paid staff member in different congregations, she has served as Children's Education Director and Adult Education Research Assistant. She has done extensive research on women's roles in the church and has spoken for retreats, seniors' meetings, and teacher training sessions. Her hobby is acting with community theater.

"A remarkable first novel"

—ANNIE DILLARD

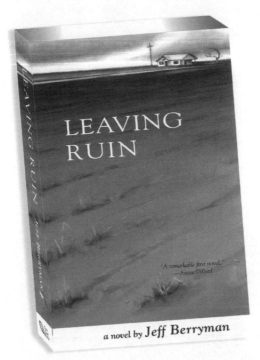

" *Jeff Berryman has taken an evangelical preacher, and turned him into the most unexpected thing: a human being. A remarkable first novel.*"

—ANNIE DILLARD,
Pulitzer Prize-winning author
of *Pilgrim at Tinker Creek* &
Holy the Firm

"*An exuberant romp through the territory of the spirit that has as many laughs as moments when it pulls at the heart.* Leaving Ruin *embraces the life of the religious and lets it sing with humor, pathos and, ultimately, true significance.*"

—ALBERT HALEY, author of *Exotic: A Novel* (winner of the John Irving First Novel Prize); writer-in-residence, Abilene Christian University

JEFF BERRYMAN is a writer, actor and director whose original one-man performances have been seen across the United States and Canada. He has toured the stage version of *Leaving Ruin* extensively, as well as other dramas. Jeff lives in Seattle, Washington.

---

360 pages $13.99 paper $19.99 cloth

Ask for it at your favorite bookstore
or call toll-free 1-877-634-6004

New
Leaf
Books

REACHING UPWARD

Prayer evangelism.

At first look this phrase may seem to combine two very different tasks. Prayer is primarily communing with God. Evangelism is proclaiming the crucified and risen Christ to the world. How would we mix these two practices?

That question is the focus of this inspiring and practical book. Born out of the author's experience and rooted firmly in Scripture, this book provides specific ways for churches to develop a prayer ministry focused on reaching lost people.

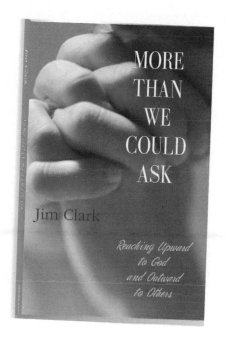

"If you cherish words like 'comfortable,' 'predictable' and 'manageable,' be slow to pick up this book. It should be marked DANGEROUS. For when we decide to depend on God, to listen to God, to obey God and to come before God in prayer, life gets risky. He does more than we can ask or imagine. As the minister of the church where Jim Clark and his family belong, I've seen firsthand the power of what he's witnessing to in this book. This book—a splendid weaving of theology and testimony—comes from a devoted Christ-follower who practices what he preaches."

—MIKE COPE, Highland Church of Christ, Abilene, Texas;
author of *One Holy Hunger*

JIM CLARK serves as response minister and writer for Herald of Truth Media Ministries in Abilene, Texas, and is the author of a devotional book, *Daily Courage* (1999).

---

160 pages $10.95 paper

Ask for it at your favorite bookstore
or call toll-free 1-877-634-6004

New Leaf Books

54757